Not The Blue Book

Dave Jones

GW00566838

THE BRITISH PUBLISHING COMPANY LIMITED

First published by Dave Jones © 1997

Second edition (revised) © British Publishing Company Limited 2006

Published by The British Publishing Company Limited, 33 St Michael's Square, Gloucester GL1 1HX
www.british-publishing.com

Printed by Pensord, Tram Road, Pontllanfraith, Blackwood NP12 2YA

ISBN 0 7140 3811 3

This revised edition has tried to give advice and guidance in the light of changing riding conditions on the roads in the UK where ever-increasing volumes of traffic and higher performance vehicles provide greater challenges to the advanced motorcyclist. Never has the need for advanced riding been so necessary to cope both physically and mentally with the driving habits and attitudes of the average motorist.

Not The Blue Book

Not the Blue Book is a practitioner's guide. Various books on advanced motorcycling explain topics without telling the ordinary rider what he needs to do, when to do it, or indeed, when not to do it. Read on to find out more about the do's and don'ts of advanced riding, but remember you should only attempt a manoeuvre when you are confident, competent and concentrating. Any advice given here is purely for information. No responsibility is accepted by the author or the publisher, and throughout it is assumed that readers will already have attained an above average ability.

About the book

This book lists thoughts and actions to be considered when motorcycling through various hazards. It is designed to get you thinking, but, more importantly, thinking sooner. By doing this you will have created more time to carry out your actions, which will result in a safer ride. It is based on years of experience and riding in all weather on all types of machines, coupled with the extensive theoretical knowledge gained on several police training courses. 'You can only learn by experience' say some. Read and use this book to learn from another's experience.

Many riders have asked for definitive answers to simple questions; they are provided here. Where there could be more than one answer it provides one viewpoint with pointers to others. You may have already developed a method of carrying out a particular manoeuvre, in which case adjust the points offered in this book to suit your needs.

Use it as a reference book. Begin with a mental picture of a location you know, then use any suggestions from the book you could benefit from. It contains exercises you may wish to try. Only attempt these when you fully understand what you hope to achieve, and are confident about carrying them out.

Where there is a numbered list, another one follows explaining the reasons behind each item. Item one relates to reason one and so on.

About the author

Who is Dave Jones? He served 30 years with Dorset Police, the majority of that time as a motorcyclist. He qualified as a police motorcycle instructor in 1977, and during his training received some of the highest marks ever awarded at the regional police driving school. After a police teaching course in 1980 he was fully prepared for the years ahead.

He became a member of the VIP Escort Group giving service to heads of state, foreign dignitaries and royalty. He was part of the nine-strong team tasked with producing the 1996 edition of HMSO's **Motorcycle Roadcraft: The Police Rider's Handbook.**

His own motorcycles have included BSA, Triumph, Yamaha, Honda, and BMW. He currently owns three.

Police machines have been Triumph, Norton, BMW, Kawasaki and Honda.

His other publication, **The Assessment of Advanced Motorcycling,** is a guide to how well you are doing, where each section is divided into 'Essential' or 'Desirable' categories. Only when all the 'Essential' elements are satisfied can riding begin to be classified as advanced. By adding some of the 'Desirable' elements the standard is improved still further.

Contents

Definitions

Straightening out
Taking the straightest course, but remaining on the left of any centre lines.

Life-saver
A last check over the shoulder prior to being committed to a manoeuvre.

Filtering
The passing of other vehicles travelling at less than 30 mph in a queue(s) which would not be possible in a car.

Rear observation
Knowing what is behind. Can be by mirror(s) or over the shoulder.

Concentration
The full application of mind and body to a particular endeavour to the complete exclusion of anything not relevant to that endeavour.

Space for the ace
A gap in a line of traffic ahead which you can comfortably occupy having come from another lane. Preferably without having to brake.

SSV
SAFETY - STABILITY - VIEW. Primary objectives with all positioning, and always considered in this sequence.

Safety position
The safest position for the machine to occupy in relation to dangers existing or apparent at that moment.

The lurker
An opposing vehicle partially or completely hidden behind a larger one.

Hazard
Any circumstance or set of circumstances that will cause the rider to consider changing course or speed.

Reaction time
The time that passes between the moment a rider sees the need for action and the moment he takes that action.

The blue book
HMSO's **Motorcycle Roadcraft**.

Blind spot
An area to the side and slightly behind the rider which cannot be viewed by use of the mirror(s).

Cutting in
Pulling too closely in front of a vehicle you have just overtaken.

S.T.U.D.D.
Abbreviation for Sense, Think, Understand, Decide, Do.

Observation
To see and at the same time to register in the conscious mind what one has seen.

Actual danger
Where the law or rule of the road places the onus on the rider to ensure it is safe before continuing. (Probable late gear change.)

Potential danger
Where common sense or road sense suggests certain safety precautions be taken before entering the danger area. (Probable early gear change.)

Introduction

Motorcycles are promoted by their ability to travel swiftly. Many standard showroom machines are capable of accelerating faster than some of the most prestigious sports cars. A machine responds through its controls, which are operated by the rider, it only does what the operator tells it. Unless there is a major malfunction with the machine, which is very rare these days, the rider is the one in control. Control the rider, and the recipe for exhilaration, enjoyment and satisfaction is complete. Unfortunately, to the average motorist, motorcycles appear to be dangerous, excessively fast, noisy, and to blame for everything that happens on the road. They also assume the riders of such machines have the same characteristics. An advanced rider therefore has a difficult job, to prove to himself he can ride well and convince others that their initial impressions are unfounded.

Motorcycling is a complex activity. Riders tackle many hazards at the same time: one physical feature, such as a roundabout, may hold further hazards of a poor road surface and circulating traffic. This book does not attempt to describe the correct way to negotiate a particular hazard or collection of them, but covers each activity associated with the manoeuvre. A rider rarely has difficulty with one manoeuvre in particular, such as a roundabout, or right turn, the difficulty is normally with a component activity, such as observation or positioning. The sections of this book aim to provide information on each component activity, which is then applied to whatever manoeuvre is being attempted. First you use OBSERVATION, followed by S.T.U.D.D., POSITIONING, SIGNALLING, SPEED, GEARS, and OVERTAKING. The book uses these as section headings.

Analyse these sections to find where any deficiencies lie in your riding and make adjustments accordingly. Such a comprehensive guide has not been produced before; use this for an insight into the thinking behind advanced motorcycling. If anything is unclear, you should seek advice from an instructor or examiner before attempting the manoeuvre. Rider training is generally available throughout the country, your local police force should have details. Pay them a visit or search their website for more information.

Before You Ride

Clothing

No recommendations are made for a particular product or manufacturer, you should seek advice from a reputable supplier.

There are certain essential items which will be required before setting out on the road in addition to the legally required safety helmets and visors.

Injury results from:
1. Impact with a solid object.
   (The transfer of energy to the body generally results in fractures or contusion, the speed of impact governing the degree of injury.)
2. Abrasion along a solid object.
   (The skidding generally results in laceration and abrasion injuries, the extent being governed by the coarseness of the surface and length of time in contact.)

Protect yourself as best you can:
1. By having energy absorbent material in either the machine's or clothing's construction.
2. By having abrasion resistant clothing. (You cannot alter the type of surface you may skid along.)

Being uncomfortable is distracting. You cannot afford distractions so take some time to decide on the clothing type that suits your riding. A mainly summer/fairweather rider may choose leathers and an unlined lightweight waterproof oversuit whereas an all year round rider may prefer a suit made from a waterproof membrane like 'Gortex' which provides warmth and coolness. This style offers the option of wearing anything from just a t-shirt to thermals and a pullover underneath.

Boots should give support to the ankles as they are constantly flexing. Give some thought to spending just that little extra for some waterproof membrane boots as they avoid the need for overboots when it is wet.

Gloves should always be worn.

If it's raining before you set off, remember one thing before you put your waterproofs on: take the ignition keys out of your trouser pocket!

When did I last ride a motorcycle?

Ask yourself this question, and if you cannot remember when you last rode you should be using the first few miles to re-familiarise yourself with the bike and its capabilities. So many riders put their bikes away for the winter and the first sunny weekend of a new year get it out and try and ride like they did the previous autumn. It cannot be done, however good you think you are. Remember that car drivers have not seen motorcyclists for several months and are also unused to making assessments of their speed and distance when one appears in sight after five months' absence!

I have dealt with many riders during springtime where they have either been involved in crashes, were not riding very well, or were speeding simply because they were a bit rusty and did not take a little time to get back to peak performance.

Training

Motorcycling has been subject of many legislation changes over recent years with compulsory theory and practical training followed by tests becoming our way of life, but once the licence is obtained and larger bikes can be ridden it is left to the individual to take further education.

You have embarked on this route by reading this book and as the saying goes 'knowledge is power'. But this is only true if you use it. A big advantage motorcyclists have over other drivers is that they want to be educated. So many do not rely on their bikes for everyday use, just for pleasure, and the more pleasurable the experience the greater the appeal.

Post-test training is available countrywide and there will be a scheme somewhere to suit you. It is a fact of life that there is always someone who knows more or can ride better than you - seek him out and use his expertise to improve your own. Local road safety offices, the internet, or telephone books can provide a starting point.

Track days and off road riding

These are also widely available, using your own machine or a hire bike. Track days allow you to explore cornering and braking limits in a relatively safe environment. They can improve your appreciation of what your motorcycle can actually do (and, just as importantly, what it cannot!). Off road days are particularly valuable to develop confidence and machine control.

Observation

This requires 100% concentration. It is the foundation upon which all good riding is based. High speeds sap concentration, and long journeys should be broken or well within one's riding limits.

Even though you may be expert at handling your machine, the rider with better observation skills will make more progress, smoothly and unobtrusively. If you have ever had a crash, or heard about someone else's, and later had the sense to try and work out what went wrong you might have identified a point at which that crash became inevitable. Prior to this point there were probably clues as to what could have prevented the crash. A lot of observation is about seeing these clues and interpreting them. Maybe there were skid marks on the road, someone was braking before they disappeared from view, there was a dog bouncing around in the back of a car as it neared a park, or a hundred other things. First you must be concentrating, then you must be looking, then finally all you have to do is take the hint something is about to happen. Battles are often won by using the element of surprise, make sure you don't lose the battle of survival having been surprised by something that was foreseeable.

The 'advanced' in advanced motorcycling comes from doing things earlier, which can only come from seeing them earlier as the following examples demonstrate.

Forward observation

This must include to the left and right. You not only need to know what is in front of you now, but also what will or might be there in a moment.

Approaching junctions from a minor road

The general motto for all junctions, especially roundabouts is: **AIM TO GO BUT PLAN TO STOP.**

- Try to keep rolling whenever possible, unless approaching a STOP sign. By keeping rolling you can adjust speed up or down easily and keep control of following traffic.
- Look right and left along the major road as soon and as often as possible. Get early clues of traffic patterns. Can you see along the road you are about to enter, see any obstructions, traffic, pedestrians, which may affect your decision to turn, or an approaching large vehicle which may cut the corner turning right into your junction?
- Check traffic on the main road, its density, speed and any usable gaps. This will influence your next actions. This traffic may prevent you pulling out - adjust speed early to try and keep rolling. It may turn into your road, so ensure there is a safety margin should it make a wide turn. If it is busy, with no gaps, you know in advance you will have to wait at the junction. If there is a gap available you can plan to arrive at the junction at the right time.
- A regular fault is approaching too fast and not having time to take these lateral observations in advance of the junction. Take time, by reducing speed, to develop the skill and the speed will soon build up again.
- Vehicles overtaking on the major road regardless of the junction are a danger, your job is to see and avoid them. If you are turning left, remember to look left for these overtakers before emerging.
- If following another driver, he may not be as proficient and could slow down or even stop, despite your knowing it is clear to proceed.

Approaching junctions from a major road

The items below mostly relate to when you intend making a turn, but some are equally important if you are going straight ahead.

- Hatch markings may invite opposing traffic, as well as following traffic, to overtake. Rear observation is crucial.
- Look into the minor road as soon as possible. Can you see along the road you

are about to enter, see any obstructions, traffic, pedestrians, which may affect your decision to turn? Is the turn tight or the road narrow which will affect the position or speed? Can you overtake a vehicle waiting to turn ahead of you immediately you enter the minor road? By keeping rolling it allows a smoother turn. When going straight on at junctions look for vehicles approaching from the minor road. Avoid arriving at the junction at the same time. Is anything likely to be affected by your intended change of course or speed? Rear observation is essential.

- If a vehicle is waiting at the minor road junction always assume the driver has not seen you, even if he is looking in your direction. Adjust your approach position and speed accordingly until you are sure he is going to wait. If that vehicle is prevented from emerging by other traffic you are much safer.

- If you are the only thing preventing that vehicle from making its turn be especially careful, especially those waiting to turn right across your path. If you have vehicles in front of you think about closing up behind them on the approach rather than slowing down. Although you reduce your visibility to the emerging driver you and the car in front become one object and it provides your protection. There is safety in numbers.

- If the waiting vehicle is large it may take a wide sweep as it turns left out of the junction. If there is no opposing traffic make a conscious decision whether to hold back and allow it to make its wide turn or not. Rear observation is crucial. If there is opposing traffic it prevents the lorry from emerging, but be watchful for any headlight flashing from opposing vehicles. This can be a difficult balancing act between being able to stop, thereby encouraging the vehicle to pull out, and the danger this may create for following traffic, Try and have an ever evolving plan to keep yourself safe.

Roundabouts

If following another driver, he may not be as proficient and could slow down or even stop, despite your knowing it is clear to proceed. Look at traffic patterns and decide which is the best lane to be in.

Signs giving warning of a roundabout can give more than just destinations. (See illustration at top of page 33)

1. You always approach a roundabout from the 6 o'clock position on the sign.
2. Look at the thickness of the line that forms the 6 o'clock approach. If you are on the most major road your line will be thickest.
3. If you are entering from a dual carriageway, look to see if the line showing your exit is the same thickness and shows the dual carriageway continuing.
4. Identify how many junctions you have to pass before reaching your exit.
5. Identify which are the major roads passing through the roundabout.
6. Identify all the exits, and not just those labelled with destinations on the sign.

How does this help?

7. You always have the same start point on every sign.
8. The busiest traffic will be on the major road(s), shown by the thickest lines. Your entry road may flow quite quickly onto the roundabout, with drivers using local knowledge to speed things along.
9. A dual carriageway continuing into your exit may allow a choice of perhaps 3 lanes on the approach. If the sign shows an end to it, expect congestion at the exit and plan accordingly. (Here the advanced rider can appear to have already reacted to something that has not come into view.)
10. If the roundabout is large or busy it may be difficult to keep a good look out for the destination board required. By simply counting off the junctions life is made much easier.
11. If you are not on the major road, be prepared for the busier route containing more and probably faster traffic.
12. Your signal must be based on the layout of all exits.

When on the roundabout remain alert to others:

- Any vehicles alongside are dangerous. You rely on drivers' lateral vision, but they will be concentrating on their route and exit. You become invisible. Additionally you can probably take a straighter course through the roundabout, but you must ensure it is safe to do so. (See Overtaking, page 48.)

- Danger may lie with other vehicles you became aware of when you first checked, but a large expanse of roundabout on either side could suddenly house a fast car. Identify them early, deal with them as they are reached, do not wait for something to happen and react to it.
- Look into your exit as early as possible, sometimes this can be done on the approach.
- If the exit road is open and straight, earlier acceleration and a straighter course may be possible. Any obstructions or vehicles to be overtaken can be planned for on the roundabout. (To the untrained eye you will appear to have reacted to something that cannot be seen.)
- If the exit provides a worse situation than normal, such as a parked milk float or lorry unloading, early positive action will be required. Signals for this new, and to most, unseen danger, are essential for your own welfare. Think survival. If following drivers fail to react to the signals, then abort the exit and go round again.
- As you become proficient at straightening out roundabouts you must be prepared for drivers joining them to be surprised at your pace. You must be prepared to stop if necessary, despite having right of way. Be aware that the legislation governing roundabouts can be complex, especially regarding compliance with circling painted dots and vehicles on the roundabout having priority whether they are on the left or right. If you do not know the rules look them up or ask.
- Identify foreign vehicles, especially lorries where the left-hand driving seat gives them little, if any, observation to the rear and offside. These drivers often drive with no signals around the outer edge of a roundabout to reach their exit, or keep circling until they have made a guess.

Forward observation generally

Urban riding
- Look well ahead, despite your low speed.
- Observe the whole scene. Try and anticipate what everyone is doing or about to do.
- Identify hazards and put them in order of importance, the most dangerous being the most important and so on.
- Apply the S.T.U.D.D. principle, (see S.T.U.D.D., page 17).
- Choose a position to follow other traffic which gives the best views and maintain them by changing course and speed where necessary. (See Positioning - The distance at which to follow, page 22.)
- Store information as it appears, bus route, dustbins out, concert date today.

Rural riding
- Look ahead as far as you can see. Views of distant towns, roundabouts etc may be available for just a moment, but can be stored for later use.
- If the road disappears left or right, look across in the same direction and look for:
    clues to help with judging bend severity;
    any obstructions or opposing traffic;
    changes in the centre white line system which might permit overtaking;
    road signs showing a further hazard or junction.
- If the road disappears over a brow, look to the left and right and judge which is the more likely direction change by looking for:
    buildings, open fields, rivers etc., all of which tend to indicate it is not in that direction;
    hedgerows, telegraph poles, street lamps, all of which indicate it could be this direction.
- If this reveals nothing check the surrounding countryside to gauge the amount of gradient to expect.

Rarely does the road enter a sharp deviation with no warning, look for the clues.

Observation links
Once you have observed something it is invariably linked to something else.

By successfully linking these together your riding becomes much safer, better planned, smoother, and eventually faster. Not necessarily by miles per hour but progression. Providing a complete list of observation links is impossible but here are a few to think about:

- You are following a brand new car, it's a base model and has 2 occupants or more - it's probably a hire car driven by a foreign driver used to driving on the right.
- You are following a car with a tow bar and 2 electric sockets, it's not a local registration number - it's probably a caravanner on his way back to a local campsite, look for the campsite signs.
- Car in front has a trailer loaded with rubbish - it's probably going to the tip.
- Vehicle in front has horses in a trailer or a horse box - it's going to the local gymkhana.
- The agricultural tractor in front has a trailer so big you cannot see the tractor - it's only on a short journey and will turn off into an obscure entrance absolutely anywhere.
- The ambulance holding the traffic up ahead is travelling quite slowly - it's probably going to turn into the hospital entrance.

These are just a few basic examples, but they all contain elements providing the essential ingredients for linking observations and planning what MIGHT happen next.

Overtaking early
(Repeated later under Overtaking)
In a line of traffic where you are some distance away from its head, watch for any vehicles ahead overtaking. This could be useful. Use the driver's eyes, and any skill he might have, to assist in the decision to overtake as well. His vehicle is a shield. He will avoid any oncoming traffic for his own survival, or he will show a brake light should he abort. As long as he is about 4 vehicles ahead, you maintain a safe gap, and gain time to react. Once again other drivers in the queue will not be aware of the safety of this manoeuvre and think you have a death wish, overtaking where you cannot see very far ahead.

If you are not confident with this - seek a demonstration from someone who is.

Motorways/dual carriageways
- If you are joining a motorway or dual carriageway via an overbridge, look down onto the carriageway you intend to join. It may have queuing traffic, an abnormal load, an accident or be completely clear. All this information is required before joining the slip road, as you will then be committed to entering the main carriageway.
- If joining from beneath the main carriageway look up for the speed of the traffic, it may be just a queue. You may decide to take an alternative route.
- Avoid looking over your shoulder checking traffic on the main carriageway whilst riding round the left hand bend onto the slip road. If a motorist has stopped on the slip road you will crash into him.
- If the slip road traffic is moving slowly try leaving a gap ahead of you before reaching the main carriageway, your blending in may be much safer. It reduces shoulder checking, entry is achieved by speed increase not reduction, and provides a safety margin should the driver ahead hesitate at the last moment.
- When on the main carriageway watch the wheels of vehicles ahead for any movement towards a lane line, this tell-tale sign precedes the lane change itself. Do not expect the driver to use an indicator, your advanced observation has received a signal already.

Remember the advantage of moving to a vacancy in a nearside lane when an offside lane is just a queue of traffic. It gives a perfect view of much further ahead, allowing much better planning. (See Positioning later).

Rear observation
When you intend to alter course or speed you MUST know what is going on behind, not just what is there. (See Definitions - Observation.) Only the foolish fail to keep their rear observations up to date. Not only can they save your life, but also your licence. Most of the speeding offences I detected were by simply following the speeding rider or driver and they simply failed to observe me behind them!

Mirrors

Mirrors are invaluable for saving lives, especially your own. Whether you love them or hate them, use them, and often.

If they vibrate at a particular engine speed:
- Mirrors fitted to handlebars - tighten your grip.
- Mirrors fitted to fairings - check the foam pad between the fittings.

Know exactly how much can be seen through both mirrors - areas that cannot be seen are 'blind spots'. Use shoulder checks to see into these when necessary. (See Shoulder checks, page 14.)

Glass in mirrors can be plain, convex or concave. Each gives a different reflection - be aware of what is fitted on your bike, and whether images appear to be closer or further away than normal. Remember this if borrowing an unfamiliar machine.

Mirrors should be spotlessly clean - why?
- They will vibrate.
- They are only a few centimetres square.
- They show an area that can be hundreds of metres away.
- An object or vehicle behind may only cover a small area of the mirror.
- Dirt on a mirror may disguise or even hide such a vehicle.
- You may react to what you think is a vehicle, but is actually dirt on the mirror.

Mirrors and training:
To assist with mirror use and develop regular usage whilst under training, try to put them both slightly out of adjustment. You will need a slight movment of the head to get the full rearward picture, so the instructor is left in no doubt that a mirror check has been done.

Develop regular usage by following these guidelines:
- In busy urban areas, where speed is low and traffic compact, mirrors can play a smaller part than usual as so much activity is taking place ahead and to both sides. Check every 7 seconds, when safety permits.
- In urban areas where traffic is flowing they become more important. Check every 7 seconds, but make time available to ensure these checks are done.
- In rural areas, in the national speed limit check every 10 seconds.
- On dual carriageways check every 10 seconds.
- On motorways most danger comes from behind, check both sides at least every 10 seconds. (Remember 70 mph is 105 feet/sec. so 10 seconds represents approximately 350 metres.)
- When waiting at a junction and checking left and right, scan through the mirror as your gaze passes it.
- This scanning should also occur whilst looking around in roundabouts and a series of bends. (See Forward Observation, pages 10 and 11.)

Advantages over shoulder checks:
- A mirror is positioned in front of you, in your normal field of vision.
- You can notice movement in the mirror, even if you are not specifically looking there at the time.
- Similarly, if you are looking in the mirror and something changes in the road ahead, you will see it.
- A quick glance can be used before losing a good long distance view before a corner or hill brow.
- If something occurs ahead requiring immediate action, the mirror provides the initial safety check without affecting stability, vision, or control.
- It passes through the field of vision when looking left or right, and can be scanned in passing.
- There is no loss of vision in forward or rearward directions when it is being checked.

General usage:
- Most vehicles have to be fitted with mirrors.
- Always try to be in a position to see into the mirrors of the vehicle ahead - if you can see him he can see you, (if he chooses to). This is even more important when behind lorries and other large vehicles.
- Britain is the only country in the western world that drives on the left. Any foreign

registered vehicle drivers are at a disadvantage when driving here, remember this and allow for their lack of visibility.

- If the vehicle ahead has the sun visor down, the driver is unlikely to look in the mirror. Be alert to this and assume he does not know you are there.
- When filtering, the mirror is the only rearward observation required. You will be travelling down a tunnel of traffic, with your blind spots occupied by stationary or slow moving traffic that should cause no concern. All danger comes from ahead and alongside.
- Check the mirror and take in the information, try not to waste time by checking again shortly afterwards when nothing could have changed.
- If a driver ahead is waiting to cross your path, check the mirror first. If he can cross a couple of vehicles behind, do not waste his and your time by inviting him across in front. He will have seen the gap and planned for it, do not upset his plan.
- Your mirror use should be such that, if an emergency situation suddenly occurs in front of you, you can safely assume the situation behind you has changed very little from the last time you checked, and can take evasive action in relative safety. To change course or speed without such information could be disastrous!
- When you ride faster than your brain can cope you naturally omit certain actions to reduce the load and rear observation is the first thing to go. Beware of this in your own riding and when following others who are travelling 'fast'. There is always a tendency to think 'no one is travelling faster then me'.

The fact is: **fast riders forfeit rear observation - do so at your peril.**

Shoulder checks

Advantages over mirror checks:
- A motorcycle is only about a metre wide, most road lanes on two-way roads are about 3 metres wide, and a car is up to about 2 metres wide. Therefore a car can travel on the same side of the road and be alongside a motorcycle. If this happens it will be in your blind spot. Blind spots can only be checked by looking over the shoulder.
- If you intend to adjust position or speed and have a vehicle following closely it can fill the mirror and mask any further vehicles that could affect you. A turn of the head can give the following driver a clue you are about to do something. Also, remember this clue should you see another rider doing the same.
- A change of lane in busy traffic often requires quite a large deviation in a short distance. Only a shoulder check can provide the essential view.
- In towns, cyclists can creep up on you despite frequent mirror checks. They can only be spotted by shoulder checks before moving off or changing position.

General usage:
- Use them before occupying a section of road that may house another vehicle in your blind spot(s), (e.g. the straight course through a roundabout, a lane change in traffic, or before actually turning across a lane, as in a right turn).
- Use it as a communication point with the driver behind before you suddenly change course or speed.
- You may have to make a 'lifesaver' check earlier than normal if the view ahead is limited and opposing traffic could come into view suddenly and affect your decision to turn.
- If under training, it may be useful to include them on a regimented basis. It ensures a rear observation is taken at the correct time and the instructor can see it being done. It also builds in some extra time before a manoeuvre is carried out, which can assist a trainee to develop his skills.
- Precede a shoulder check with a mirror routine, checking both first. This acquaints you with everything around you. This is especially useful when undergoing training.

Some publications give a variety of names to the business of looking behind. When you have identified the need for such a look, you will know what you are looking for, and therefore where and when you should be looking and which shoulder to use.

When not to use them:
Looking over the shoulder means the view ahead is lost for up to 2 seconds. In that time, at 30mph 27.4 metres (90 feet) will be covered, at 40mph, 36.6 metres (120 feet) and at 60mph, 54.8 metres (180 feet).

Don't use a shoulder check:
- When the hazardous picture ahead is so busy that no time can be given to looking behind.
- When there is nothing to see (e.g. in a country lane when turning left).
- When nothing can physically get into a blind spot (e.g. turning right from a lane guarded by pedestrian rails that you are alongside, or from a reservation on which your right foot is resting!)
- When the speed at which you are travelling causes the visor to lift or your head to catch the wind and wrench your neck.
- When the change of position can be done by a gradual deviation, and the time taken permits adequate mirror use to cover the blind areas.
- When you are lead vehicle waiting to emerge into a major road and you are fully aware of what is happening behind. (It creates dangerous time after your last check of the main road and things could change before you emerge.) (See Mirrors, Advantages over shoulder checks, page 13.)
- When you have approached a right turn major to minor, opposing traffic is heavy, your approach speed has been slow in order to gauge your turn without having to stop, and you have been monitoring your mirrors. Your turn takes place immediately after a vehicle has cleared your path, and there is no space on your right from which a vehicle could suddenly appear, (e.g. view behind covered by mirrors, blind spot occupied by traffic.)
- When you are entering a dual carriageway or motorway from a slip road and have not checked the slip road ahead for obstructions, slow moving vehicles or a queue.

Shoulder checks take time - can you afford it? - are you travelling too fast?

(See illustrations on pages 33 bottom and 34 top.)

Rear observation - general usage

Approaching junctions from a minor road
You must know what is going on behind.
- Check for anything likely to be affected by your intended change of course or speed.
- Check for responses to signals you have given.
- As your speed and/or position changes, check for responses from following traffic.
- If you require more time to carry out a manoeuvre, make sure following traffic is responding.
- Check for cyclists, or other motorcyclists, who may have crept up unnoticed and may affect your planned turning angle or speed.

Approaching junctions from a major road
You must know what is going on behind.
- Make a full assessment of how much notice and what signals are likely to be required.
- Check for anything likely to be affected by your intended change of course or speed.
- Check for responses to signals you have given.
- As your speed and/or position change check for responses from following traffic.
- Check any blind spot(s) which may contain danger before committing yourself to the turn.

Roundabouts
You must know what is going on behind.
- Check for anything likely to be affected by your intended change of course or speed.
- Check for responses to signals you have given.
- As your speed and/or position change check for responses from following traffic.
- Always check it is safe to occupy another lane if straightening out a roundabout.
- If a shoulder check is necessary before leaving a roundabout it will often be better to look sooner, probably while the machine is more upright at the penultimate exit, rather than a lifesaver, when it will be more difficult to take an alternative course.

Night time rear observation
Moving motor vehicles cast light well ahead at

night. This effectively makes any rear approaching vehicle as large as its light beam which will extend through any blind spot(s). Shoulder checks can become unnecessary.

Where you may conflict with smaller road users, such as cyclists who have no such light, the blind spot(s) still has to be checked.

Restraint

One disadvantage of advanced motoring is that it heightens awareness of bad driving and riding by others. This can lead to frustration and the path towards ever-increasing 'road rage' incidents. It is therefore essential to use all your advanced skills to avoid becoming entangled in these drivers' antics.

Most people simply use vehicles as a means of transport or business and have no inclination to improve their driving, sometimes not even to government test standard. We have all been passengers in vehicles driven by friends, relatives or colleagues, they are really nice people and they would do anything for anyone but just cannot drive a car to save their life. It can sometimes ease your frustration with other drivers if you imagine the 'offending driver' is one of those people that you know.

S.T.U.D.D.

Unless you abound with natural ability you will need to adopt a systematic approach to dealing with any hazard. There are a number that have been developed over the years but the object remains the same, to consign a lot of the thought process involved in complex situations to automation. This leaves you with more free brain to evaluate the information you receive and make decisions. Remember when you learned to ride, you had to look at the clutch to make it work? Now your left hand and foot change gear without even asking you. The same applies to a system, when your brain says 'brake' your right hand and foot won't act until your eyes have looked in the mirror. Which system you choose is not important as long as it works for you. There will always be some aspects that will logically appear in a particular order, such as a rear observation before any change in course or speed, but the important point is the system is committed to memory. This will complicate your riding in the short term, some trainers will get you riding round the block until you can recite the features backwards! However you achieve it, the aim is to be able to draw upon the parts you need without consciously thinking. This achievement may involve you having to adjust your system and use all the features on all occasions just to memorise it. At the end the system works for you and then you use only those parts that are needed.

Sense, use touch, smell, sound and sight.
Think about what you have just received from your senses.
Understand what it means.
Decide what all those involved are likely to do, including yourself.
Do what you decided was the best plan.

Motorcyclists have advantages over car drivers.
- They sit higher off the ground, and are therefore able to see more.
- They are in the fresh air and can see, hear and smell more.
- Their vehicle is smaller and more nimble.
- They are under constant threat from other motorists and must concentrate more.
- Most are also car drivers and have a greater degree of road sense.

S.T.U.D.D. explained

Use concentration and on most occasions you can know something, and start dealing with it before most car drivers. The principle is applied throughout your riding. Think about it. This is the process you go through every time you deal with a hazard.

Similar in many respects to observation links, this principle extends and expands into areas available only to motorcyclists, and then only the advanced ones.

Sense
1. Smell the newly chopped hedgerow.
2. Feel the rear wheel twitch.
3. Hear the siren of an emergency vehicle.
4. See the brake lights on a car just disappearing around a bend in the distance.
5. If you taste the tarmac, return to page one.

Think
1. This smell only occurs when hedges have been recently trimmed.
2. The road surface may have appeared adequate when you last looked at it closely, what has changed?
3. There is an emergency vehicle in the vicinity.
4. Why is the driver braking?
5. Where is page one?

Understand
1. There is probably a hedgetrimmer around the next bend causing an obstruction.
2. This might be a diesel spillage or a frosty area, more attention to the road surface is required.

3. It will be travelling fast, some traffic will be taking avoiding action, others will obstruct it.
4. You will probably have to brake as well and may join a queue of traffic just out of sight.
5. Hospital patients have lots of time to read books.

Decide

1. The hedgetrimmer driver will be concentrating on the hedge, not the traffic. If it is on your side of the road there may be a queue behind it. If it is on the other side, traffic will be overtaking it, and be on your side of the road. You must be FULLY aware of what is behind and be able to stop in the distance you can see to be clear IN PLENTY OF TIME.
2. This is only the beginning. Stability is priority.
3. Where the emergency vehicle is coming from. That other traffic immediately nearby are aware of it. You must have a safe piece of road to use should it suddenly appear.
4. To remain visible to any following traffic. To give advanced warning of unexpected speed loss. To have an escape route.
5. I am not going to do this again.

Do

1. Check behind by mirrors more frequently. Reduce speed. Be ready to stop around the next bend. Remain vigilant to following traffic not yet in view. Surprise everybody by showing you are already prepared for the sudden appearance of a hedgetrimmer.
2. Become more stable by smooth adjustments of speed and/or position. Look for a better surface. Expect more poor surfaces. Warn others if you can.
3. Keep checking all around. When it appears or you are certain where it is, make your way to a safe position which will allow it to pass. Sometimes you may have to speed up not slow down. Watch the movements of others.
4. Check behind more frequently by mirrors. Reduce speed well in advance. Adjust braking to ensure you remain visible to following traffic, either present or expected. Consider brake light and arm signal benefits.
5. Do your best to avoid it happening again.

Positioning

A motorcycle is most stable when it is upright and travelling in a straight line. The more often it can be kept in this state the better.

Some riders adopt a different riding style when the road is wet because they fear the lack of adhesion. As long as you do not wish to overcome the rules of physics and ask things of your machine that are not possible, try selecting courses you would use on a wet road surface when it is dry, where there are few direction changes, speed adjustments, gear changes and drain covers, then when it rains you need not change your riding style. In that way your riding remains in your 'comfort zone' come rain or shine.

Positioning is based on **SSV: S**afety, **S**tability and **V**iew, (see Definitions). Safety will always take priority, followed by stability.

Quite often you will need some degree of view and will continually seek out the best one available before deciding on the optimum position. Once there is a reason for not adopting that position it should be given up. Positions may also be given up if they are likely to be confusing, misleading, or of no advantage.

Junctions

Riding in pairs

When riding as a group, junctions can become a major hold up if everyone queues one behind the other.

If turning from a minor to a major road, the lead rider should arrive at the junction in the normal position. The second rider should position alongside, but on the opposite side to the intended turn. Any others should form up behind likewise. Do not obstruct any vehicles which could move along the nearside to make a left turn. Two riders at a time then have the same view that can lead to them exiting together, and it halves the length of the queue.

Forming a two abreast group to make a right turn major to minor road can be dangerous. Only attempt it in exceptional and well-controlled circumstances, where ALL riders can be adequately protected from all other traffic, such as hatch marked areas. This shorter queue is bulkier, more visible and is the same width as car.

Use the same principles in traffic queues at junctions

If you have filtered along a queue leading to a junction, and the lead vehicle is a car, a similar principle can be applied. A position alongside it but the opposite side to its intended turn can often be adopted.

- Ensure you do not block the driver's view, and never put yourself in a position where you are relying on his view alone to exit.
- Allow the car to go first, the driver has been waiting the longest and a motorcyclist stealing the 'first away' slot will do nothing but annoy him. If you choose to go in the same gap ensure you leave space and time should that driver be slow away.
- At major to minor right turns where traffic is protected by lane markings (see Overtaking - Filtering, page 49 and Overtaking on diagonal stripes, page 51) and a queue has formed, try positioning just behind the driver's position of the lead vehicle to obtain the same advantage. This may be on his offside or nearside depending on the layout of the junction. (Great care is needed for this manoeuvre.) Once again, do not try and be 'first away' unless offered the place or alongside a milk float or similar.
- At left turns minor to major and roundabouts, where your view to the right is obscured by a larger vehicle waiting to turn right, you can probably make your left turn safely when it makes its right turn. Ensure you remain shielded by it until you are able to cope with

any approaching traffic without its assistance. You will hear the loud bang in plenty of time if another vehicle collides with it, and be able to take avoiding action.

- When waiting on the offside don't obstruct traffic turning into the junction. You may have to wait further back to allow larger vehicles access into your road.

Approaching junctions from a minor road

Position towards the intended direction of turn. For a right turn towards the centre of the road, for a left towards the nearside, (remember SSV). This allows other turning traffic to come alongside, but only if YOU wish them to. If not, position accordingly. If the road is narrow, traffic entering your road may need more space, adjust your position accordingly. In one-way streets, gyratories and dual carriageways join into the closest lane, matching speed in a slip road if possible. Sometimes this could be lane 2 or 3, beware of other traffic changing lanes.

Approaching junctions from a major road

- Position towards the intended direction of turn. For a right turn towards the centre of the road, for a left towards the nearside, (remember SSV). This allows other traffic to pass alongside, but only if YOU wish them to. If not, position accordingly.
- When turning right, position to be visible to as many road users as possible. The more drivers who can see you the more chance there is of them co-operating. Help them to help you. If it is not safe to adopt such a position find an alternative. (See Riding in Pairs, page 19.)

Compliance with junction markings

The subject of cutting corners at junctions when turning right has been discussed for many years. Other than straightforward breaches of the law a motorcycle is only normally on the 'wrong' side of the road AND travelling in the 'wrong' direction when it is overtaking. Turning in and out of junctions puts the machine on an angled path across the other side of the road, not along it. There are basic thoughts that need to be applied to this controversial subject:

- Traffic on major roads travels faster than on minor roads.

- Traffic leaving a major road has to reduce speed to make the turn into the smaller road.
- Traffic entering a minor road does not have to blend in with other traffic and can proceed at its own speed.
- Traffic entering a main road has to cross one lane before being able to merge with the intended direction traffic.
- Views into a minor road are often only obtained when a rider arrives almost at the point of turning.
- Road surfaces on minor roads are not as good as major roads and are worse at junctions.
- Traffic on minor roads has an obligation to give way.
- Traffic on a minor road has two directions to monitor at the same time before emerging.
- Views along a major road are essential before attempting to join it.
- A motorcycle is most stable when it is upright, travelling in a straight line, with the engine pulling the load.

Major to minor

Cutting the corner into a minor road is unnecessary.

Reasons:
1. You have to be in control of the situation behind, normally by your position.
2. You have to slow down to make the turn.
3. Traffic could appear on the minor road and force you to adjust your plan(s). So plan to comply.
4. The view into the junction is often limited and road surface poorer.
5. There is no traffic to match your speed to.
6. The turn is a manoeuvre controlled by limited and late views of traffic and road surface.

Overtaking a vehicle turning into the same junction is however sometimes possible and desirable. In this case you would go straight into the offside of the minor road, get the machine more upright and apply acceleration.

Minor to major

There are advantages to be gained at SOME junctions by marginally cutting across the centre junction marking.

Reasons:
1. All traffic must give way, and may have to stop.
2. More time is required to check both directions before pulling out. The views along the major road are normally good, and being almost stopped provides this time.
3. You have to cross a traffic lane before gaining the correct side from a slow speed, and you must match your speed to other traffic to merge with it.
4. You have the time to check the road surface and can expect an improvement once on the major carriageway.
5. An overtake directly from the junction would be unusual on a motorcycle, as long distance views would be necessary well in advance of the actual junction.

Be careful if you carry out any non-standard manoeuvre.

Roundabouts

Left and right turns are covered in many publications, and compliance with the accepted rules governing them should continue. Don't forget to read the sign(s), especially where a dual carriageway is involved, as more than one lane may be available for use. (See Forward observation - Roundabouts page 10.).

Traffic circulating a roundabout rarely signals to continue circulating. This is very apparent with foreign visitors and extra care should be taken with them.

Avoid being alongside another vehicle at any exit, you cannot be sure which exit it is going to take.

Where a more or less straight across exit is the intended destination there are several advantages to taking a straighter course. These are:
• Greater stability due to a more upright position.
• Safer position, away from vehicles waiting to emerge from intermediate exits.

Things to LOOK FOR before straightening a course are:

1. Lane selection may be dictated by road markings, comply with them.
2. Once on the roundabout, have no vehicles alongside you.
3. Before making a move towards the exit identify the danger areas(s).
4. If not done on the approach, look into the exit as early as possible.

Reasons:
1. Every driver can comply with the markings, and most do. Do not be an unknown quantity to others by selecting wrong lanes just for that extra bit of progress in moving traffic. (But see Filtering, page 49.)
2. Any vehicles alongside are dangerous. You rely on drivers' lateral vision but they will be concentrating on their own route and exit. You are therefore invisible. Additionally you can probably take a straighter course through the roundabout than them, but you must ensure it is safe to do so. (See Overtaking, page 48.)
3. Danger may lie with other vehicles you became aware of when you checked at 2 above, or a large expanse of roundabout on either side that could suddenly house a fast car. Identify them early, be prepared to alter course, do not wait for something to happen and have to react to it.
4. If the exit road is open and straight, earlier acceleration and a straighter course may be possible. Any obstructions or vehicles to be overtaken can be planned for on the roundabout. If the exit provides a worse situation than normal, such as a broken-down vehicle or lorry unloading, early positive action will be required. Extra signals may be required. Think survival. If following drivers fail to react to the signals and you are at risk, then abort the exit and go round again. Never think because you aborted the manoeuvre you have failed to deal with it properly. It will give you more time on the next visit which will be much safer.

The advanced rider can normally get into a position to take the straightest course through a roundabout by adjusting speed and position on the approach, then, by using a little acceleration just prior to entry, leave others marginally behind, but checking over the shoulder before occupying the other lane. This straight course is not restricted to the approach, some roundabouts are so tight that straightening is only possible on the exit, in either case a check over the shoulder is essential. (Also see Overtaking and Observation.)

Be ready for changes in the camber of the road, they are designed to assist drainage as well as traffic. They can cause your bike to flip up or down with very little or no advance warning.

Mini roundabouts

These are often just blobs of paint on the road surrounded by at least three arrows pointing clockwise.

Know the law regarding the correct route round the roundabout.

It is an offence to fail to comply with the arrows and circle the roundabout clockwise.

See the advice given in Signals and Roundabouts - Signals to exit, page 29, where a signal may not have time to flash before you have exited the roundabout.

The distance at which to follow

You already know what is a safe distance at which to follow other traffic, advice is widespread in The Highway Code, The Blue Book and many others. Apply this to motorcycling, knowing your machine is about a metre wide and your height from the ground is greater than most car drivers, both of which are distinct advantages.

In addition to the safety aspects, position to gain the further advantages of:
- Views under, over, or through the vehicle in front.
- Views along its offside and nearside by slight deviations.
- Being able to stop safely should the vehicle in front brake suddenly (assisted by the observations gained above).
- Providing more time for a following vehicle to stop, by extending your own braking distance.

- Having space available for acceleration prior to moving to the offside for overtaking.

When travelling in a queue on a rural road you may be able to use vehicles further ahead to provide assistance with overtaking, see 'Overtaking Early'.

Where a driver ahead brakes every time an opposing vehicle appears, treat him with extra caution and allow a greater following distance.

Reaction time

(See also Things You Didn't Know You Didn't Know, page 55.)

This is one of the most overlooked processes in all driving and riding. Concentration is a key element here and if good observation provides a clue that a hazard may be developing it can greatly reduce reaction time when something needs to be done.

When REACTION TIME is occurring, distance is being covered. This distance is the THINKING DISTANCE.

When you are THINKING you are not ACTING. At crucial times the need is to ACT not THINK.

Things which affect reaction time:
1. Physical condition.
2. Mental condition.
3. Degree of concentration being applied.

Caused by:
1. Illness, hangover, allergy, fly in the eye, coldness, etc.
2. Depression, age, brain overloaded by information.
3. Distracted by domestic issues, next appointment, punctuality, mobile phone.

Plus, thinking distance increases with speed.

Unfortunately you only ever see a vehicle's speed, not the driver's condition which is the more important aspect. Do not assume every driver is as alert as you.

Adopt the view he is ill, depressed, on the phone and travelling too fast.

Night riding

- Many things change when night falls.
- Some features become less dangerous yet others more so.
- Your greatest enemy at night is the road surface, especially on an unlit road.
- Headlight range is poor, and by the time you have perceived a need to take avoiding action for something in the road it can be too late. Travelling in the tyre tracks of the vehicle ahead can put the mind more at rest.
- Be aware of your limitations and those of your bike in respect of its lights and braking.
- Text book positions for view are of little use. They rely on illumination and there is rarely sufficient.

Making use of others

- A vehicle ahead illuminates the road well in front. You will see signs, bends, debris, in plenty of time.
- A driver even further ahead, or at the head of a queue, may dip his lights, signifying an opposing vehicle. Conversely, such a vehicle putting lights on main beam may signify no such vehicle.
- An opposing vehicle's lights cast a sheen of light along the road, highlighting any undulations or debris to be avoided.
- Vehicles, other than a pedal cycle, cast a light ahead of them, which is easily seen before the vehicle itself appears. If approaching a junction on the left, use this advantage to position closer to the nearside should you wish to. Similarly it may assist overtaking near offside junctions, conscious you will see the light before the vehicle.

Urban riding

Urban riding requires a smooth progressive yet unobtrusive riding technique. Some of the positions adopted are not featured in any text book, they are often simply for survival.

- Safety remains the primary factor, a position being rarely adopted for view alone because speeds are generally low and close to the speed limit, and overtaking, other than filtering is not generally possible.

- You may find gaining a view of as many brake lights or indicators on vehicles ahead will give you a clue when traffic is slowing or intending to turn. Whether this is a nearside or offside view will depend on which side the junctions are ahead. Do not adopt a position which invites any following traffic to come alongside you unless you want them to.

General positioning will normally range between the centre of the road and centre of your side of the road, this keeps control of following traffic which may be tempted to overtake should you position to the nearside for no apparent reason.

When coming to a halt in traffic, leave enough space in front to be able to ride around the vehicle in front, especially at traffic lights, where the driver in front often waits for the red light to change to green before indicating.

Adopting a proud position in 30mph areas is acceptable for marked police vehicles, as they are there to enforce the limit. Trying to adopt a similar position on a civilian machine will attract more danger caused by frustrated drivers, and will have little effect on controlling their speed.

Positioning for safety means putting yourself further away from danger, therefore any position adopted with a reduced safety margin will require a speed reduction.

Changing lanes

Where a choice of lane is available, select the best one based on observation, anticipation and planning. If the situation changes you should re-assess the selection and change lanes if necessary. Do not be reluctant to change lanes, if the initial assessment was sound, criticism can only be given for not changing lanes to meet the new circumstances.

These changes require little change of speed. If a change is required, acceleration is far better than braking, there is less need to consider the motorist behind who may be busy looking for direction signs. (See Signalling - Changing lanes, page 28.)

Rural riding

Use good observation to anticipate possible developments ahead.

For instance, where the road bends left and an opposing cyclist comes into view think 'What happens next?'. Normally a vehicle appears from behind the cyclist, travelling at the speed limit or greater, partially or completely on your side of the road and unable to stop before reaching the cyclist. You can do nothing to prevent this happening. Every time you see such a cyclist simply position away from the centre of the road. This way, even if the erring motorist does not appear every time, you are always ready for him when he does.

(See illustration at bottom of page 34.)

Wet roads

See the opening paragraphs of this section for general advice on positioning on wet roads.
*   Take a little more time to manufacture spaces in traffic which will allow you to ride more upright.
*   Extend distance observation and allow more time for others to react to signals. Extend following distances.

As the road dries out a dry alley forms between tyre tracks. This may be the best place to ride on despite it being 'out of position' for text book purposes. Remember SSV.

Crossing centre lines

A subject hotly debated. Where the road ahead has a centre line (see Highway Code definition), and has a series of minor bends to the left and right yet all the road surface remains visible, there are campaigners for adopting a course which takes them across this line to maintain a straight course.

I campaign for riders to straighten within their correct side of the road.

Reasons:
1. There are many occasions when other traffic in the vicinity can be misled:
    *   Opposing drivers may believe you have not seen them, and brake.
    *   Following drivers do not know what is about to happen next, and brake.
    *   A following rider will imitate on another occasion, not knowing when it is safe or dangerous.
2. Opposing traffic initially unseen is confronted with a vehicle on its side of the road for no reason, and brakes.
3. The extra degrees the machine is kept upright are only marginal.
4. The extra speed this may provide is minimal.
5. If the position is essential for stability I suggest the speed is too fast in the first place.
6. The extra stability provided is minimal.
7. If the next opposing vehicle to appear is an emergency vehicle on a call, urgent repositioning may be required by both drivers (see Overtaking page 46).
8. Motorists are possessive about 'their side of the road' and are prepared to fight for their territory if necessary.

(See illustration at top of page 35.)

Where there is no centre line, use whatever position is safe. You are not on 'their side'. Remember SSV.

The distance you position out is dependent on the view ahead and width of road, as these increase so can the speed, but bear in mind the potential problems listed above can occur here as well.

On single track roads where debris gathers in the middle it will be difficult to change tracks quickly. Being closer to the left often outweighs the slightly earlier view.

Motorways and dual carriageways

Returning to the nearside
1. Return to a nearside lane if you would

spend at least 10 seconds in that lane before needing to move out again.

2. This may have to be modified if there is fast closing traffic behind.
3. If lane 3 traffic is cruising at a constant speed, is nothing more than a queue and only passes vehicles in the nearside lane(s) occasionally, a move to a nearside lane can be useful at times.
4. If there are pedestrians standing on an overbridge, especially children, and you can avoid passing directly under them, do so.
5. Stay in the outside lane(s) for longer in heavy rain, and when lorries have begun to bunch together.

Reasons:

1. This will give sufficient time for any following traffic to overtake, or show they do not wish to. It also allows for any mirror checks in the new lane to establish the new traffic pattern. (See Rear Observation, Mirrors and training, page 13.)
2. Fast closing traffic may require you to clear their path sooner. It should take them less than 10 seconds to overtake and you can pull out again when it is clear.
3. The vacant lane gives a perfect view of much further ahead. Brake lights, lane changes, road debris, and traffic signs can all be seen earlier. Maintain a slot alongside you in the outer lane, it will permit movement out when you reach the next vehicle to be overtaken. There will be far more space available, and a number of alternative plans can be formulated should an emergency arise. Being in a queue where the speed can change suddenly is dangerous.
4. People throw things off bridges. To them it is fun. The heavier the object the less distance it can be thrown. Plan for them throwing something, do not wait for it to happen.
5. Spray can mask you from others. If you can see through it, pass quickly. If you cannot, take a wider berth. The risk is from two motorists not knowing the other is there. Headlight use may be helpful. Switch it on, do not flash it, (remember what lorry drivers think headlight flashes mean).

Avoiding cats eyes

If, as a trainer or instructor, you discover a rider who thinks he knows everything and can ride fast as well, give him this simple extra task to do. It is not related to speed and he will become embarrassed if he cannot do it. It is designed to give his brain extra work which will induce a natural reduction in speed.

- Avoid riding over cats eyes when overtaking or changing lanes. Initially this is difficult, as the more concentration applied results in more being ridden over than avoided. The secret is to concentrate on the centre of the gap between them, you tend to ride where you are looking. This simple exercise can also help him avoid drain covers and debris in the road with little deviation, extending his observation.

Once this has been mastered, get him to cancel his indicators between flashes. Having the bulb illuminated at the time they are switched off is not acceptable. This may frustrate him even more as it is a simple task but it does keep his mind working at full capacity.

Signalling

Timing of signals

You should be a thinking rider and consider signals based on the actual conditions, not signalling automatically without thinking.

Indicator

At what point a signal should be given is very important.

It is not the distance away from the manoeuvre that is important, it is how long it will take you to get there. Signals must always be signals of intention, not of achievement.

Important factors to consider:

1. How many road users need to see the signal? Answer: the more there are, the longer the signal.
2. How great is the speed loss/increase going to be? Answer: the greater the change, the longer the signal.
3. How close is the following vehicle? Answer: the closer it is, the longer the signal.
4. How large is the following vehicle? Answer: the larger it is, the longer the signal.

Reasons:

1. Each driver needs time to react to a signal. Provide time for each of them.
2. Drivers do not like having to slow down for others, they prefer to overtake. Keep them under control, ensuring they do what is best for you. Tell them your intention, they don't know what you are thinking until you tell them.
3. You need to provide a safe braking distance behind you. An early signal can help.
4. Large vehicles take longer to stop. The driver is higher off the ground and may see your signal late, despite it being given in plenty of time.

Any combination of these requires the signal to be carefully monitored. Give it early and look for reactions to it.

When to give them

If the only consideration for the giving or not giving of a signal is following traffic, use this as a guide. A following vehicle can be defined as:

- At 30mph, within 100 metres.
- At 60mph, within 200 metres.
- At 70mph, within 300 metres.

Always indicate a change of direction, i.e. for turning left or right.

This signal may only be considered unnecessary in the following circumstances when all these conditions are met:

- No traffic in view behind.
- No opposing traffic in view.
- No traffic in view in a junction.
- No traffic able to come into view before you are carrying out the turn. (It is better to have an existing signal operating than to have to give one late.)

Indicators flash at least once a second. You must provide sufficient time for others to react to them. Drivers need time to react, (see Reaction time, page 22), therefore time is the important factor, not distance. As a guide, allow:

- At 30mph, 12 flashes to occur before
  i. crossing the junction line (left turn major to minor road), or entering a slip road.
  ii. reaching the point of turning (left or right turn minor to major, and right turn major to minor).
- At 60mph, 15 flashes.
- At 70mph, and on motorways, 17 flashes.
- When overtaking, 3 flashes before the wheels are on the offside of the road, or in the next lane.

Try this yourself, adjusting the timings to suit your riding style or needs at the time. If you have difficulty seeing the indicators to count the flashes when moving, check their flash speed when stationary and count at that speed when you are riding. This develops the important skill of judging the distance at which you should begin your signal.

As a general guide, on rural roads, the primary route sign is about the right distance at normal speeds.

Reason:
A signal is for showing an intention. It is no good showing a signal when you are already carrying out the manoeuvre.

Travelling faster requires an earlier signal, (i.e. further from the junction). Remember, at 60mph you cover a quarter of a mile in 15 seconds.

Motorway exits can be congested, with several drivers attempting to use the same piece of road. Some indicate their intentions, others do not. Those who indicate can be given more precise judgement, if you are indicating you can be similarly judged. This can help avoid the free for all that often occurs as the slip road arrives. Allow for some who may change their mind.

Cancel a signal when the activity it describes has been completed.

If the signal is to change position, when the change is complete, cancel the signal. If it is to turn, when turning has finished, cancel the signal. It is good practice to cancel one signal, and give a second or two delay before applying another for others to realise you have a further intention.

One-way systems and gyratories

If it is clearly a roundabout, signal according to guidance on roundabouts. (See Roundabouts, page 28.)

Most one-way and gyratory systems have a lane marking arrangement, either on the road surface or overhead gantry.

These systems rarely require a signal on approach. (See Changing lanes, page 28.)

If you are unable to position in the correct lane when joining, perhaps because signs or markings were obscured by traffic, attempt to be in it no later than any penultimate exit, it may help you avoid having to signal to exit.

Do not assume those joining the system know the lane markings, they are new to this piece of road and must be given time to read and respond. Think ahead to avoid coming into conflict. Just think if it were you in a strange town trying to find your way round, how would you wish to be treated?

Local knowledge is a useful aid to town riding. Give others extra room, more time, and additional signals if necessary.

A signal to exit will be required if:
• The selected lane allows you to go in more than one direction.
• There is no physical barrier such as bollards or kerbing to ensure you can only go in one direction.
• Other traffic could be in doubt as to your intended exit.
• Other traffic has an obligation to give way to you and your intended route is not clear to them.
• A pedestrian is waiting to cross the road on part of the system you will not be using, and he is unsure of your route.

Even though a lane is marked clearly with your intended route, other road users will be looking at you, not the road marking, for confirmation of your intended exit.

A signal is not required if there is no choice of direction, such as joining a dual carriageway or one way system.

(See illustrations on pages 35 bottom and 36 top)

Returning to the nearside

(See also Motorways and dual carriageways, page 29.)

In the UK traffic drives on the left. The assumption must be that all traffic will return to its left once any manoeuvre has been carried out. A signal is not normally required for this natural assumption, and any traffic in the new lane will be travelling slower than you and will be left behind.

Changing lanes

Where a simple change of lane is required, and does not form part of overtaking, a signal is rarely required.

It is not required if:
- It can be done by a slight or gradual deviation.
- Traffic in the new lane is travelling slower than you.
- There is no following traffic.
- There is no other road user who requires it (e.g. a pedestrian ahead waiting to cross).

To pull away

Pulling away should not cause anyone to alter course or speed, therefore a signal is rarely required.

Reasons:
1. If there is no one there to alter course or speed there is no need to signal.
2. If there is no suitable gap to pull away you wait until there is.

A signal may be required:
- Where there is constant traffic and you must rely on another's courtesy to let you pull out.
- When pulling out from a lay-by on a dual carriageway and traffic could use the right hand lane but is not.

Think of the indicator as being a request for a space in the traffic. If no such request is necessary, nor is a signal.

Passing an obstruction

Obstructions are stationary objects. To continue on your given path you may be required to go around an obstruction. A signal would not be required to pass an obstruction that is clearly visible to all road users.

If there is any doubt about its visibility, consider a signal, but it is unlikely to be required.

The brake light

A brake light comes into operation when the lever or pedal is applied, not necessarily when a reduction in speed occurs. This can be useful.

It is not good practice to show a brake light to a following motorist who is simply driving too close.

Only when you intend to alter your course or speed should it be considered, not just to encourage him to drop back, but to provide him with extra reaction time (thinking distance) which could be vital to your survival, (see Reaction time, page 22). Any driver who is uncomfortably close should be allowed to pass when you decide it is safe. Alternatively, by overtaking the vehicle in front, you leave him to bother the car you have just overtaken.

When approaching an unexpected traffic queue such as on a motorway, a rhythmic operation of the brake light could attract more attention than an arm signal. This would be preferable if speed reduction were required at the same time as a signal. Exercise caution to avoid sudden changes in speed that can cause instability to you and surprise to following drivers.

Remember a driver's behaviour for survival is often: **a crash appears inevitable, brake (no mirror check), if this will not work in time, swerve around the obstruction.**

As the driver gets closer to the end of the queue, if he realises he is not going to stop in time he will change lanes. Watch for drivers doing this ahead of you, more importantly, be aware of it happening behind and prepare to take action.

Signals and roundabouts

Signals on the approach and for exiting a roundabout are mainly dependent on the layout of the roundabout and the traffic circulating. To help you plan, there are generally two options available: read the sign, or use local knowledge.

(See illustration at bottom of page 36)

Approaching

The advance warning sign for a roundabout often provides information for deciding what signals are required. Use this as a guide in the first instance.

Treating the roundabout as a clock face, with you entering at 6 o'clock:

1. If the exit you require is significantly after 12 o'clock a right turn signal is required on the approach.
2. If the exit you require is the first, signal left on the approach.
3. If the exit you require is both 12 o'clock and the first, either indicate left on the approach or give no signal at all.

Reasons:

1. This makes your intended path a turn to the right, your speed through the roundabout will probably be slower than others who are going straight ahead, they may be able to overtake on your nearside. (See Roundabouts - Overtaking, page 48.)
2. There can be no confusion as to your intended exit.
3. Any traffic entering from the 12 o'clock direction can be reassured that you are not going to circulate to the 3 o'clock exit, as so many drivers do without a signal. This will maintain their flow and cause any traffic approaching from the 3 o'clock position to give way to them, thus allowing you to enter the roundabout sooner.

If the layout differs from the sign

The layout is more important than the sign. The layout is real, the sign is a guide. If the roundabout does not coincide with the sign, signal according to its layout. This could mean cancelling a signal already in operation or giving one previously considered unnecessary.

The better rider is the one who sees the need for action and takes it.

If at any time there is a need to give a signal because something has changed, give it.

To exit

Do not confuse exit points with entry points on a roundabout. You cannot always exit a roundabout on a road you can enter it by and vice versa.

A signal to exit is only required if you will pass an exit prior to the one you want.

This signal should be given after the penultimate exit point, and when the machine is alongside an area it cannot use to exit the roundabout, for instance:

- The start of kerbing between exit and entry points from a dual carriageway or motorway.
- Beyond the centre line of an entry road immediately preceding your exit.
- Beyond the centre line of an entry road that is followed by an entry point only (i.e. is 'No Entry' for traffic on the roundabout).

If the roundabout is so small, or speed so fast, that a signal would not have time to operate or have any meaning, do not give it.

Once you have mastered the basics there may be occasions where you can give an earlier signal where there is someone who could benefit and nobody to confuse. These situations rarely occur but can help maintain a safe smooth ride when perfected.

Motorways and dual carriageways

- Timing of signals is fully explained earlier. (See When to give them, page 26.)
- Motorways and dual carriageways contain drivers who are concentrating more on the view ahead than behind.
- Always signal any intention to move to the offside when there is following traffic. (See When to give them, page 26.)
- On 3-lane motorways signal an intention to move right when there is traffic ahead or behind. (Traffic ahead is looking for a space to move in to, your signal identifies one about to be created.)
- Headlamp flashing is a constant activity amongst bus and lorry drivers. Generally it is to tell the overtaking driver it is safe to return to the nearside. Be aware of any headlamp flash being misunderstood.
- Remember a signal is to show an INTENTION. Signal first, check for responses, then move. On motorways

especially, drivers signal at the same time as moving, be alert to this.

- At the beginning of a dual carriageway, if no change of course is necessary to enter the offside lane, no signal is required.
- Signals to join motorways are only required if there is traffic on the slip road or on the main carriageway.
- A signal to move to a nearside lane is normally only required when you need to join heavy traffic which is travelling at a similar speed to yourself. Think of it as being a request for a space.
- Be alert to any traffic in lane 1 likely to move into lane 2 at the same point you wish to from lane 3. Remember a signal in this situation is easily missed and gives you no right to the space you want.
- Be aware of the ineffectiveness of motorcycle indicators in congested traffic and adjust your riding plans to allow for those who may not have seen them.
- On leaving a motorway or dual carriageway by a slip road where you intend to turn right ahead, select a course to take you straight into the right hand lane, thereby avoiding a separate lane change and the need for a signal to adopt it.

Sounding the horn

At times the visual flashing of your headlight will be more effective than the audible horn warning, especially at speed or at night. The advice that follows applies to both, but beware of the possible misinterpretation of a headlight flash.

Reference books state a headlamp flash is to tell others of your presence. Not everyone uses it this way. If a headlamp is flashed always think there is more than one meaning.

You make a conscious decision to sound the horn, it does not happen accidentally, it is not caused by some external source like a gradient. Once the button is pushed the sound comes out, there is no turning back, you cannot turn it down and hope it was not noticed. To decide when a horn warning should be given is therefore important. First seek alternative plans if

possible, give a wider margin, slow down. This may be all that is necessary to make things safe, making a horn warning unnecessary.

Use it:

- To attract the attention of others who need to know you are there, (e.g. children playing near the road, cyclists, drivers at roundabouts).
- Where the view ahead is very limited and the road is narrow.
- Prior to overtaking if you require the attention of the driver about to be overtaken, (e.g. on a country road where he may deviate slightly).

(See illustration at top of page 37.)

Arm signals

Arm signals are so rare these days that any seen are often a surprise, bear this in mind. When you need someone to pay more attention to what you are doing, consider an arm signal. Make it clear, make it in good time, and do it when you can afford the time to do so. Do not be embarrassed to give them, be proud, make them effective and clear.

An arm signal would be required:

- If you are the lead vehicle approaching a pedestrian crossing where someone intends to cross, (regardless of following traffic).
- If you intend taking an exit or junction which is not clearly identifiable by all and there is following traffic.
- Where following traffic could be misled into thinking you are overtaking, not turning right.
- Where following traffic is so close you need to create a safe gap behind you before reducing speed.
- Where you intend to reduce speed for something you do not believe following traffic is aware of, (horses etc.).
- Where you intend to slow down to a speed which following traffic would not expect, (diesel patches etc., as they mean nothing to car drivers).
- Where you intend to stop at the side of the road. A slow down arm signal has only one meaning, an indicator has three.

- If you intend turning left into a minor road where another vehicle is waiting to emerge, and the only thing preventing it from emerging is your presence.
- If there will be a great speed loss that will affect following traffic, such as a right turn from a fast road.
- If an indicator may not be seen due to bright sunlight, (i.e. shining on the indicator or in the following driver's face).
- Where, by experience, you have found the indicators on your machine are not as efficient as you would like, and they need support.

- If there is a sufficient gap just a few vehicles behind you the driver is probably preparing himself to go then, do not throw his plans into disarray, it will take a lot longer than you planned for him to emerge.
- If the driver is strange to the area, foreign or simply inattentive it will probably be ineffective.
- A slow down arm signal would be the best option as it gives information to all drivers, and it shows exactly what you intend to do.

Flashing headlight

The Highway Code gives clear guidance on this subject, but in reality how many drivers abide by it? Very few, so what should we as motorcyclists do about it?

Using any signal which may be confusing is dangerous, only you know the true meaning, and you cannot assume the recipient agrees with your thoughts and intentions.

Lorry and bus drivers flash headlights to indicate when the faster vehicle has cleared the slower one during overtaking, a common and accepted practice, but only between those groups of road users. Once a different user type becomes involved, so can the confusion.

The roads of Britain have become a place where courtesy is a rare commodity as everyone is in a rush and the attitude of 'you're first - after me' generally applies. The motorcycle occupies a small space on the road and it would not be expected for its rider to allow others to go before it. If a car drivor is waiting to emerge from a junction do not use a headlight flash to let him out, there are a number of reasons:
- If you have following traffic your machine is an insufficient barrier to control them and prevent then pulling out around you. The drivers could not be given the same information, as they cannot see your headlight.

Speed

Deftness in operating all the controls of a motorcycle is a skill which will contribute greatly to the smoothness sought by many advanced motorcyclists in their enhancement of their riding performance. Nowhere is this more apparent than in the use of the throttle. The power available from a modern sports machine is phenomenal and the advanced rider should seek to use this with forethought and planning, riding almost as if a pillion was always being carried. Not that acceleration would be slow or prolonged, simply introduced gradually and progressively thus avoiding the 'on' or 'off' technique used by the average rider.

There are some advantages to be gained by doing this:
- There can be some advanced warning should the road surface not be as good as first thought.
- There is a greater need for advanced observations and planning, especially when overtaking, which then leads to an improved technique and greater safety.
- You receive compliments from your next pillion passenger, and a desire to travel with you again.

The quest for speed

On any advanced test you will be expected to make adequate progress. If it is safe to travel at the speed limit you will be expected to do so. While every rider may not always wish to ride like this, it is necessary to demonstrate you have recognised these occasions when they occur. Part of the advanced training is therefore focused on this aspect, and achieving the optimum level of progress is the goal of many motorcyclists.

However, this goal sometimes becomes overwhelmed by the desire to be the fastest thing on the road and a belief that no one else should be travelling at this fast speed and everything

should be overtaken. Do not be drawn into this false world of achievement.

Those who descend into this dangerous way of thinking only achieve their speed by omitting other aspects of advanced motorcycling, simply because they no longer have the time to include them. Once common sense is disregarded, where do they stop? Only when something goes wrong do they get a sharp injection of reality! The crash or the fixed penalty.

I rode an unmarked police patrol bike for eight years and most speeding motorcyclists were detected simply because they failed to check their mirrors when I followed them. None of them disputed the evidence and most reflected on how stupid they were in not regularly checking behind.

This quest for speed often arises in group runs, which are on the increase in recent years with the emergence of more motorcycle clubs and regular venue attractions. Here peer pressure can override all other considerations providing the temptation to ride beyond the rider's limits. 'Fast' is a relative term. It is usually the point at which you are unable to process and react to everything that is going on. When people talk about 'fast' they probably mean 'too fast'.

This whole process is doomed to failure from the start. Even if you live long enough to respond to all the fixed penalties and speed camera photos there will always be someone prepared to ride faster than you. So what can you do to perfect your advanced motorcycling? Perhaps smoothness is the answer - read on.

(See illustration at bottom of page 37.)

It will only come from the best advanced skills. Why you might ask. Your riding can only become smooth by the earliest identification of a need to change course or speed, through that early observation, anticipation, and planning. This smoothness, unlike the quest for speed, is an

Continued on page 41

Direction signs show more than just destinations.

Check the slip road is free of obstructions before looking over the shoulder to the right.

You do not want to be accelerating towards this obstruction whilst looking behind.

If a cyclist comes into view you must expect there to be a vehicle about to overtake it.

Being on the offside of the road to straighten these bends leaves you vulnerable to opposing high speed traffic as yet unseen. If you can travel fast so can the opposing vehicle!

Signal not required here, joining drivers are in no doubt as to the routes being taken by all other traffic.

Signal required if travelling in the left lane as a choice of left or right is available. Give the signal even if there is nobody waiting to join. You will be expecting someone to appear so be prepared, and one step ahead.

Can you spot an incorrect sign here? Answer on page 56.

This busy street scene may require a horn warning, but think about it first.

Don't be the fastest rider to the graveyard.

Lots to think about here: blind acute bend; hazard lines; poor road surface; no pavement.

Even though you could ride through this roundabout at perhaps 40mph, it would give a driver arriving at the 9 o'clock entry absolutely no chance of seeing you when he looks right. Adjust your approach speed accordingly.

You must assess the opposing vehicles' increasing speed as well as
the target's before committing yourself to overtaking downhill.

Car drivers queue and give motorcyclists opportunities to practise their filtering skills.

On dual carriageways and motorways there is often a choice of position for filtering, but which lane do you choose?

Would you filter up the nearside of this queue?

area where you can become the best. Sure, you can build up your speed once smoothness has been achieved, but as soon as things start getting ragged you will know it is time to slow up.

Acceleration

Opinions vary on how acceleration should be described.

Acceleration is used in three different ways:
1. When road surfaces are below standard, or the machine is banked well over and acceleration could cause a skid, one type is used.
2. When everything is going according to plan another is used.
3. When things suddenly change, and 1 above does not apply, a further type is used.

They are effectively:
1. Delicate.
2. Normal.
3. Firm.

By using the same terms amongst other riders, especially those under training, no confusion can occur as to what type is being described.

Deceleration

- Speed reduction is achieved by closing the throttle or braking. (See Gears, page 44.)
- When you see the need to reduce speed and braking is necessary, try to make a single application. This will obviously be based on your initial assessment of the hazard, and should it change, so might the braking.
- Use of both brakes helps to stabilise the machine and yourself, by providing an activity for arms and legs at the same time, which also helps. In emergency braking you are effectively gripping the machine firmly.
- Be aware of the effects of any combined braking systems fitted to your machine, some operate differently under severe braking conditions and may surprise you.
- When coming to a stop only put one foot down. Select in advance which one suits

you for that occasion, it shows good machine control. Often it will be the right foot, enabling you to put the machine into neutral and back into gear at will.

Acceleration sense

This is probably the best illustration and advertisement you can have of good riding. Before any deceleration check that following drivers will not require a brake light to show an intended speed reduction.

Try to practise an aspect of it at least once on every ride.
a. Choose a point where you want to be travelling at a particular speed, make it easy to start with like a 30mph marker.
b. Travel at the national speed limit and select the point at which you decide to roll the throttle closed, checking the mirror(s) first.
c. Apply no braking or gear changes and see how close you get to the target speed. When you get it right at least 5 times move on to more difficult ones, like closing up on a line of slower moving traffic, or returning to the nearside after overtaking in a line of traffic. Remember, no braking or gear changing unless necessary for safety's sake. If you take a gear to avoid showing the brake light you are only cheating yourself.

In urban traffic, to close the gap in front which often occurs when the speed limit is being complied with, and across which a vehicle may be tempted, apply a small amount of acceleration.

Closing this gap is also useful on rural roads as the turning driver may only see a line of cars coming towards him, oblivious to your presence. By becoming a part of the line you create a greater safety margin.

Avoid dabbing the brake(s) to reduce speed by just a few miles an hour, such as entering a lower speed limit area. If the sign comes into view late, only brake if deceleration alone will result in you passing the sign at more than 10mph in excess.

See also Overtaking page 46.

Continued from page 32

Speed for bends

You have probably been experimenting with how fast a bend should be negotiated. What processes do you normally go through to come up with an answer?

The speed at which you go round a bend is based on the following:
1.	Severity of the bend itself and width of road.
2.	View into and around it.
3.	The road surface and camber.
4.	Your ability and the capabilities of the machine.
5.	Other road users you are aware of.
6.	Further road users you can expect to be there.

Any one of these factors affects the speed.
1.	The sharper it is, the slower you go.
2.	A good view results in a higher speed, a poor view could hide an obstruction just out of sight. You must be prepared and be able to stop if necessary. The poorer the view the slower you go.
3.	Expect any road surface to worsen just out of sight. Shaded areas dry out slower than sunny ones, expect the change when you enter the shade. The dry line that occurs as a road dries may be the best position to adopt, although it may mean a reduced view and therefore a reduced speed. The poorer the road surface, either present or expected, the slower you go.
4.	The experienced rider can take a small machine round a bend faster than the inexperienced one on a superbike. However, each machine has its own limit which cannot be exceeded regardless of the rider's experience and ability. The less experienced you are, or the less capable the bike, the slower you go.
5.	Other drivers complicate decision making. Will they cut the corner, brake, swerve, or accelerate? They all need to be incorporated in the decision. The more traffic there is the more unpredictable it becomes, and the slower you go.
6.	The expected road users like a post office van because of a post box in view, or emerging vehicle because of a junction

sign just before the bend. Any such observation link visible on the approach means you go slower.

Most bends offer a combination of these factors. Your job will be to apply those which fit, and adjust speed accordingly. The ultimate corner speed is only available in the perfect world, where you find a gradual curve, an unobstructed view of the entire road surface and beyond, a good road surface, an experienced rider on a professional road bike, and no traffic there or expected. But we do not ride in a perfect world, so we must compromise.

(See illustration at top of page 38.)

REMEMBER. Always have something in reserve should you need to change course and/or speed.

Junctions and roundabouts

Skilful use of continued observation will provide essential information for speed adjustments.

Your joining with other traffic should not cause anyone to alter course or speed. With this in mind try to achieve the following by adjusting speed on the approach:
•	Not having to wait in the centre of a major road to turn right.
•	Being able to overtake a vehicle making a similar turn ahead immediately upon entering a minor road.
•	Matching your speed quickly to traffic on a major road. The more powerful the bike and experienced the rider the smaller the gap required.
•	Starting the turn into the new road at a speed suitable for the road surface. Not adjusting speed afterwards!
•	Not arriving at a junction at the same time as others, whether turning or not.
•	Creating sufficient gaps in traffic to permit straight courses where possible, especially at roundabouts.
•	Controlling following traffic should you see the need, such as an opposing lorry waiting to pass a parked vehicle which could be

allowed to pass it easily with only a slight speed adjustment. (Signals may also be required.)

- Using slip roads, not the carriageway, to match the speed of traffic (not the speed limit) in the lane you are about to join.
- Ensuring roundabout approach speed is slow enough for drivers arriving at the 9 o'clock entry point to see you. You must give them time to look, see you, assess speed and distance, and then react. (S.T.U.D.D.) Do not only look ahead and to the right to decide on your speed.
- If there is a warning of a junction ahead, adjust your approach speed to give any drivers waiting to turn, time to react to your presence when you eventually come into their view. Remember they need some reaction time and it is no use becoming annoyed with them because your approach was too fast in the first place.

(See illustration at bottom of page 38.)

Slow speed

Speeds near walking pace are achieved easily on some machines but not on others.

- Your slow speed riding is an essential skill when filtering, (see Overtaking, page 49).
- If the speed required cannot be achieved smoothly with the clutch fully engaged you will probably have to run the engine against the brakes slightly, slipping the clutch.
- Smoothness is achieved by varying the brake pressure not the clutch engagement.
- Avoid long periods of this as components can overheat and lose their efficiency.

Speed generally

Speed should not only be safe it should look safe.

The foot placed on the ground when stopped should be placed on its footrest as soon as the machine is under way.

For the purposes of an advanced test, when in the national speed limit, if there is a vehicle ahead travelling below that limit it should be overtaken at a suitable opportunity. If there is a line of them, each one should be assessed in turn but not necessarily overtaken individually. You should not go blasting past all of them simply because they are travelling at 57mph!

Squirrels

While we are a nation of animal lovers, to cause an accident by swerving around one that runs into the road, or braking firmly is obviously to be avoided. A minor course change is the most you can achieve safely in these circumstances. Even this may not be possible on a wet road. It will of necessity depend on the size of the animal and the likely damage or injury a collision would cause.

Remember a motorcycle is most stable when upright, travelling in a straight line with the engine just pulling the load. Changing this equilibrium causes instability. Remain stable if a collision is imminent.

When an animal, regardless of its size, runs out in front of a driver ahead expect him to brake or swerve.

How many accidents are blamed on a squirrel?

Gears

A correct gear is one that provides immediate acceleration for normal or firm use. On poor surfaces a higher gear than normal may be needed to provide delicate acceleration and deceleration (i.e. where it is unsafe to use the brakes).

These provisos apply throughout this book.

Higher gears

Can be useful on occasions:
- Second gear can be useful if pulling away downhill. It helps to gain momentum quickly where first gear would soon be expired. (Some machines only permit first to be selected when stationary.)
- When an overtake of several vehicles or a long vehicle is becoming available, one gear higher than normal secures smooth progressive acceleration with no interruption. Often useful when exiting roundabouts.

Lower gears

Can be useful on occasions:
- When filtering, to provide immediate response to a sudden change, such as the vehicle alongside deviating slightly.
- When in busy town traffic, it is no more than stops and starts, and you are constantly changing from filtering to rejoining the queue. It allows immediate movement towards the next selected position.
- When travelling downhill and speed needs to be kept in check.

One of the differences between 'actual' and 'potential' danger, (see Definitions), is that the latter normally requires an early selection of a lower gear.

A lower gear should not be selected prior to overtaking simply to avoid showing a brake light upon regaining the nearside. This illustrates a lack of acceleration sense, (see Acceleration sense, page 41).

Changing gear

Speed reduction is achieved by closing the throttle or braking.

You either change down through a number of gears immediately after speed reduction to reach your selection, (in a block), or pass through each one as speed decreases during braking, (sequentially).

When block changing it is done AFTER speed adjustment and generally with a closed throttle. The correct gear for the speed is then selected to pick up the drive. Block changes tend to occur where the terminal speed is pre determined and not likely to change.

When sequential changing it is done DURING speed adjustment and generally with brakes applied, speed is adjusted by varying the brake pressure and gears are selected as the speed passes through each of their ranges. This allows you to pick up the drive at any time during braking. Sequential changes tend to occur where the terminal speed is variable and acceleration may be required at any point during the speed reduction phase.

Using a lower gear to reduce speed is confined to poor surfaces only, where speed reduction occurs over a longer time and distance to avoid skidding, this would be too long in normal situations.

Racing up or down through the gear box does nothing for machine sympathy and simply decreases components' life, and increases costs. Think about gear changing, especially if you have a pillion.

How you change down

The method you adopt depends on the circumstances.

1. If the hazard ahead has a fixed speed for your arrival, such as a STOP sign: block change.
2. If the hazard ahead has a changing scene and arrival speed is constantly under review: sequential change.

Let me explain further.

1. Wherever a static object dictates a particular speed is required before proceeding, then speed loss is carried out in the normal way by braking or closing the throttle. That object could be:

   A 30 mph sign.
   A junction where traffic is visibly heavy for some distance.
   A queue at red traffic lights that you intend to join.

   Essentially, you know what gear will be required when you first see the hazard.

2. Whenever moving objects force constant speed adjustments to be made on the approach. This could be such as approaching:

   A roundabout where views and circulating traffic are changing all the time.
   A bend where the view develops the closer you get.
   A queue of vehicles at green traffic lights, where they move forward at varying speeds.
   Slower vehicles ahead and an overtake may be developing.
   A junction where suitable gaps may suddenly develop.

   Essentially, you cannot tell at an early stage what gear will be required when you reach the hazard, but an immediate response of acceleration must be available at every stage on the approach in preparation for any changes.

A lower gear is not selected for speed reduction, therefore make the conscious effort to change gear at the correct time and ensure you **take a gear lower and not go slower.**

If you cannot achieve this you have probably selected the approach gear slightly too early.

When changing down try not top 'blip' the throttle. To achieve a smooth change try setting the throttle at the correct rev range before pulling in the clutch. Then when the clutch is operated and the engine disengaged the engine revs will rise gently and it allows the gear lever to freely select the next lower gear with little more than gentle pressure. This can only be achieved if enough time has been allowed for the gear change. It takes some experimenting to achieve this, but once again you will notice the difference, but not as much as your pillion.

Neutral

Select neutral and release the clutch when at an extended stop, such as traffic lights which have just gone to red, or waiting to emerge from a junction where traffic is heavy and no adequate gaps are obvious. Neutral selection is more easily made just as the machine comes to a halt. Always release the clutch gradually in case neutral is not fully engaged. (Extended means 10 seconds or more.)

Poor observation leads to sudden 'stamping' into gear when it becomes clear to go. Select the gear as the potential for movement appears, e.g. the other direction lights change to amber, or a gap is seen in the distance.

If you have to hold the machine steady by use of the rear brake your planning for when to select first gear will need to be slightly early, as you will have to shuffle feet to be ready in time.

Overtaking

You naturally avoid overtaking when it is dangerous, it is part of the survival instinct. What does happen is risk taking, born out of complacency. You may have done something a number of times and nothing has gone wrong so you continue to do it, disregarding the possible consequences. Overtaking can be dangerous but only if you allow it to be.

Overtaking is about taking opportunities, not risks.

The following principles apply throughout this section.

Things to avoid when overtaking:
* Causing anyone to change position or speed.
* Being alongside two vehicles at the same time. (Meat in the sandwich, or piggy in the middle.)
* Cutting in. (Passing too close to the vehicle just overtaken.)

Some static things always affect overtaking, such as double white lines, junctions, road width, but the mobile ones can be summarised as follows.

Things to assess before overtaking:
* Speed of the vehicle(s) ahead.
* Speed and distance of opposing traffic you can see.
* Could a fast opposing vehicle suddenly come into view?
* Speed of your machine and its performance.
* Space for the ace. (See Definitions page 4.)

Riders treat the unseen fast vehicle with too much complacency. I have ridden and driven emergency vehicles, that often come into view at a speed faster than you expect. Always think it will be that next vehicle and allow yourself that essential ingredient of advanced riding: Time to react.

If you identify that the driver in front of you also wishes to overtake, by his driving manner or type of vehicle, and you see an opportunity developing, assess whether or not that driver is also in a position to see and take the same opportunity. If so, allow extra seconds for him to do so. This avoids a collision which might occur when you are alongside or if he pulls out very close in front.

Overtaking is not a race, the vehicle in front is already ahead and its driver may have equal ability and seeks to progress exactly the same as you. You may find they can make your overtaking easier so sit back and watch for a while, also, you may have a similar admirer behind you, but do not become focused on them when you should be looking elsewhere.

There are more opportunities for you to overtake than for car drivers. In frustrating circumstances such as when queuing behind a tractor, you can show extra courtesy by allowing a car driver in front to overtake first. The opportunity to overtake him will no doubt follow soon afterwards. Once you decide to overtake him a headlight or horn warning might be required.

Overtaking early

(Repeated earlier under Observation - Forward.)

In a line of traffic where you are some distance away from its head, watch for any vehicles ahead overtaking. This could be useful. Use the driver's eyes, and any skill he might have, to assist in the decision to overtake as well. His vehicle is a shield. He will avoid any oncoming traffic for his own survival, or he will show a brake light should he abort. As long as he is about four vehicles ahead, you maintain a safe gap, and gain time to react. Once again other drivers in the queue will not be aware of your advanced planning and think you have a deathwish, overtaking where you cannot see very far ahead.

If you are not confident with this - seek a demonstration from someone who is.

Opposing drivers flash their headlights or shake their fists?

This could be for a number of reasons, but normally it is because:

- The space you have allowed yourself to complete the overtake is too small.
- It APPEARS to be too small to the other driver.

The first of these can only be corrected by allowing more space.

The second may be corrected by altering the image of your machine, as viewed from the front.

Just think what the other driver sees. A motorcycle on 'his' side of the road, accelerating 'straight' towards him. His reaction is going to be one of avoiding a collision, but without giving up any ground, he feels invulnerable inside the car and will get you to move out of the way. Change the image he sees - APPEAR to be returning to 'your' side:

- Initially move out further away from the vehicle(s) you are overtaking.
  This can provide:
  > a better view between vehicles,
  > a better view ahead,
  > a wider safety margin on the nearside,
  > a slightly longer distance to travel to regain the nearside, which can help acceleration sense practice.
- Begin the return to the nearside earlier.
  > The driver will SEE you to be moving out of his path in plenty of time.
  > You may still be under acceleration.
  > You can judge your return space with greater accuracy.

If you find your speed is marginally too fast to regain your position in the traffic without braking, this slightly greater distance of travel can help, especially if it is extended even further by continuing towards the nearside verge. This is only to assist the fine tuning of acceleration sense and is not an exercise you begin with. It is not meant as a swerving exercise, if braking is demanded, do not waste valuable time trying to avoid it - brake!

Overtaking downhill

This may seem a strange subject to include, but you need to be aware of the added complications gravity can cause.

If you intend overtaking just one vehicle there is normally no problem when you are both travelling downhill as the natural speed increases are easily compensated for by applying extra acceleration, the amount being determined by the size of the vehicle concerned.

It starts becoming difficult when there is a collection of vehicles ahead and an opportunity arises.

Think about a recent line of vehicles you came up behind intending to overtake. On the level the average speed was more or less constant, as were the gaps between them. Introduce a stretch of downhill gradient and all of a sudden the vehicles' speeds vary, the gaps alter and the overtaking conundrum begins. Invariably the gaps become smaller, which does not help with your assessment, and you can be on the offside of the road watching your intended return space disappearing and not because a driver has accelerated or braked, gravity has increased the vehicle's speed and the effect is different on each vehicle.

Now put this overtaking situation into an area where your direction and the opposite direction are heading downhill into a dip. You must calculate the possible speed increases for both directions before deciding to overtake.

You can use the opposite of course for extra benefits. When traffic travels uphill it rarely maintains the same speed, especially large or heavy vehicles. You know this will happen so you can plan ahead and make the overtake that much easier by overtaking as their speed is decreasing and yours is maintained or increasing. Even though the gaps in the traffic will vary as before they become more manageable. Your road speed will probably be lower, you will probably spend less time on the offside of the road and will have more time to think.

You may decide to practise the timing of your arrival behind such vehicles to coincide with the start of the uphill sections and reap the most benefit.

(See illustration at top of page 39)

Space for the ace

Returning to the nearside after overtaking is something we all need to practice. It is an activity forming part of acceleration sense and can demonstrate you are truly an advanced rider.

This space you intend to occupy need not be the furthest along the line of vehicles you can achieve in safety, there is more to it than that.

Look at the type of vehicle you are going to be behind when you return. If it offers poor forward views, such as a lorry, coach, or camper van, or it is throwing up too much spray for you to see ahead, or just as importantly, anyone opposing being able to see you, re-assess where you come in. You may decide to overtake one or two vehicles fewer than you can actually overtake just to achieve a better view to make the next overtake. As a general guide, think how far you would want to be behind the large vehicle if it had no following traffic and then slot into the space closest to that calculation.

In addition, assess the line of vehicles and identify the bigger gaps. Sometimes they are better to use than going for the ultimate number of vehicles to be overtaken. They provide more space for acceleration sense, but more importantly, the extra space allows for a better view of the next opportunity plus a space into which you can apply acceleration before going to the offside again. Using these larger gaps means you can often leapfrog down the line in a smooth controlled fashion, maintaining a steadier speed and rarely having to brake, something you would have to do if the gaps were smaller.

These larger gaps may be there for a number of reasons. Perhaps the driver with the large gap ahead is busy on the phone, reading the map

or simply inattentive. He may be a conscientious driver and using the 'two second rule'. Either driver will not be affected by your use of the space.

Roundabouts

Manufacturing a suitable space to enable straighter courses through roundabouts can often be further extended to allow overtaking. In well controlled conditions overtakes can be completed on the approach, whilst negotiating and on the exit.

On the approach
- Ensure the other driver is committed to a chosen course, (i.e. staying in his lane, turning left or right, braking or accelerating).
- Ensure you are able to do the opposite to him, (i.e. if he is increasing speed you decrease initially, allow him to approach first, then look for the overtake when he has to slow down).
- Ensure you are completely past him before entering the roundabout. (He, or you, may wish to take a straight course)
- Assume he is an advanced motorist and attempting the same thing.

On the roundabout
- Ensure the driver is committed to a particular course and speed.
- Check for another driver attempting the same manoeuvre on you.
- Ensure there is an escape route, especially if he changes his mind.
- Do not stray into lanes marked for a different direction.
- Always be visible to the driver you intend overtaking.
- Complete the overtake by the time you need to indicate for your exit.

On the exit
- Ensure the driver is committed to a particular course.
- Ensure he is not about to attempt the same on the vehicle ahead.

- Look into your intended exit as early as possible to ensure there is nothing that will require a speed reduction.

Use acceleration and forward vision to complete the overtake. (All danger is in front, concentrate here.)

Filtering

Filtering is the passing of other vehicles travelling at less than 30mph in a queue(s), which would not be possible in a car. Any faster traffic will be 'overtaken' and dealt with accordingly. The essential ingredient here is 'in a queue', where traffic is being held up, not where it is moving along freely at just under a 30mph limit.

Good filtering will result from the following actions:

- Knowing what is safe.
- Wanting to filter past all traffic that is queuing and travelling at less than 30mph.
- Searching for reasons why filtering CANNOT be done. Not vice versa.
- Always leaving sufficient space immediately in front when in, or approaching, such a queue.
- Presenting your machine to any oncoming vehicles in plenty of time to obtain a reaction. (If you don't get one, don't go.)
- Keeping your speed in check. The narrower the gap the lower the speed.
- Watching EVERY vehicle about to be overtaken for any suspicious movements.
- Increasing conspicuity if necessary, perhaps by switching a headlight on, or onto main beam. (Normally only necessary when between 2 lanes travelling in the same direction such as a motorway.)
- Having good slow riding skills.
- Knowing the width of your machine, and the width of gaps you are able to travel through safely.
- When carrying a pillion, use larger than usual gaps (for stability), and tell him what you are about to do.
- Reacting IMMEDIATELY to ANYTHING that appears UNUSUAL.

- Treating foreign registered vehicles with caution. The left seated driver will have a poorer view on his offside.
- Ensuring road surface direction markings are considered carefully when selecting a particular course.
- Knowing and understanding the occasions when overtaking is permitted on the nearside, as listed in the Highway Code.

(See illustration at bottom of page 39.)

Filtering past stationary traffic

- Read the Highway Code and understand when centre white line carriageway markings may be crossed to 'pass a stationary vehicle'.
- A stationary vehicle cannot suddenly pull out unless there is sufficient space in front of it. LOOK FOR SPACES.
- Watch for arms, litter, children's heads appearing from the traffic - leave space to avoid or time to stop.
- Impatient drivers may want to U-turn. LOOK FOR SPACES.
- A driver who has blocked an entrance will be embarrassed if a vehicle wants to emerge. He will do everything to assist the emerging driver, making small shunts to create a large enough gap, and then waving him out. LOOK FOR SPACES.
- You cannot see in front of lorries and buses. Stop if you have to, and look before passing.
- Road markings are designed to control moving traffic, but the only traffic on the move is you. Use the available road to best advantage, watching any opposing traffic carefully, especially near junctions.
- When the queue begins to move, identify the gap where you wish to rejoin the traffic. LOOK FOR SPACES.
- Like any overtaking, always have room to return to your own side of the road if an oncoming vehicle requires it.

Spaces are dangerous - danger means injury - injuries hurt

(See illustration at top of page 40.)

ELEMENT	ASSESSMENT	DECISION
Is it necessary? (Worthwhile)	Is it a temporary hold up and the front of the queue is already beginning to move?	STAY
What is there to be gained? (Worthwhile)	Is it a long term stop, reason unknown?	GO
	Is it a long term stop, reason known, (road works, accident, obstruction)	GO
	Is it only a short queue?	STAY
	Is the filtering difficult and the progress to be gained minimal?	STAY
Is there somewhere to go? (Safe)	Can you see where you can return to the queue should the need arise? If yes	GO
	If no	STAY
Do you travel down the offside, nearside, or middle? (Safe)	Is the widest gap the safest? If yes	GO
	If no	TAKE SAFEST GAP
	Is it legal to ride in this position?	TAKE SAFEST LEGAL GAP
Is there another motorcyclist behind? (Safe)	If it is a smaller machine it is more manoeuvrable.	HE GOES FIRST
Are there any large/wide vehicles in the queue ahead? (Safe)	View is restricted immediately in front of it.	FILTER TO IT AND REASSESS
Are there any inexplicable gaps in the queue? (Safe)	Expect an emerging vehicle, cyclist or pedestrian.	FILTER TO IT AND REASSESS
Are there junctions on the offside? (Safe)	Emerging left turning drivers will only look to their right. A driver in the queue may pull out and dash for the junction. A driver alongside it may decide to U-turn.	FILTER, but, REASSESS ON APPROACH, MAKE A MENTAL NOTE AND APPROACH SLOWLY
Is there a pedestrian crossing ahead? (Safe)	Has the foremost vehicle stopped to allow a pedestrian to cross?	APPLY RULES OF PEDESTRIAN CROSSING APPROACHES
	Has the foremost vehicle stopped solely due to the queue ahead of it?	FILTER TO FOREMOST VEHICLE AND REASSESS THE CROSSING

Filtering past moving traffic

- The slower and more compact the traffic, the easier it is to filter.
- As traffic speed increases, search for safe gaps and have one available at all times. DON'T GET STRANDED.
- Moving traffic can pull out quickly and easily, make sure you can respond with the same ease.
- Road markings require more compliance as speed increases.
- Passing through junctions requires you to be in the queue of traffic, not passing it. Do not be in the wrong lane, it causes confusion and puts you at risk.

Deciding to filter

Motorcyclists do not cause traffic jams, and consequently do not like sitting in them. Certainly on an advanced test riders will be expected to filter when appropriate so practising the technique can only be advantageous.

There are two basic questions to ask yourself each time a traffic queue is encountered and filtering is being considered:

- **Is it safe?**
- **Is it worthwhile?**

You start off by making this simple, as there are only two considerations.

If the answer to both these questions is yes, move on to the next decisions.

- **Yes I want to**
- **Yes I can** (having the ability)

If you agree with these two statements consideration is finally given to the fundamental elements.

Use the chart on the opposite page to assist with decision making. It cannot cover all eventualities but may help those who have previously considered filtering but were unsure.

It is good practice to only filter past moving traffic in lanes that are marked for your desired destination. If you become stranded in a wrong lane it is probably because you have filtered too far and have to rely on others to let you back in.

Where there are bus lanes, check the sign as some local authorities, but not all, allow motorcyclists to use them. Where there are time restrictions on their operation, allow 5 minutes extra, for the benefit of any enthusiastic enforcers who may be ahead.

(See illustration at bottom of page 40.)

Overtaking on diagonal stripes and at junctions

Clear advice on these can be found in the Highway Code. Make sure you know which areas must not be crossed.

Where such areas are in the centre of the road, bordered by a broken white line and you are considering an overtake that would entail you crossing them, consider the following:

- Identify the dangers which have caused them to be put there.
- Ask yourself 'Would I overtake here if there were no such markings?'
- Know the Highway Code's advice.
- If they are at the end of a dual carriageway, use them only to overtake much slower or heavier vehicles, (i.e. ones with limited risk of sudden changes in course or speed).
- If they are at the start of a dual carriageway, use them as above or where there is a risk of being boxed in by following traffic. Be aware of any riders/drivers carrying out an overtake coming from the opposite direction.
- If they are simply to separate traffic and make the road width appear reduced, treat them as a hazard warning line. (Ensure you know the guidance in the Highway Code regarding 'Hazard Warning Lines'.
- If they are used to link central islands, as in urban ring roads, treat them as hazard warning lines.
- If the road surface is wet remember they will be slippery.
- Do not assume you are the only person entitled to, or capable of using them.
- When another motorist ahead is overtaking, ensure he cannot deviate into premises or a turning.
- Beware of extra debris on the road as these areas are not normally driven over.

- Sometimes they are painted around small or mini roundabouts to reduce speed of circulating traffic. Treat the area as a potential slippery surface but in most cases it can be ridden over to maintain a more upright riding position.
- If they are to protect turning traffic be especially careful.

If the junction is on your left, only consider riding over them to overtake when:

a. There is NO opposing traffic, (they have the right to use it); AND

b. No driver ahead is turning left, (the driver immediately behind will pull out round him); AND

c. Any vehicle waiting to emerge is prevented from doing so by the traffic in front of you AND no driver has the opportunity of letting him out by virtue of space or speed.

If the junction is on your right, only consider riding over them to overtake when:

a. The vehicle in front cannot make the right turn by a last minute swerve or braking, i.e. he is committed to going straight on; AND

b. There is no traffic in or approaching the junction on the minor road; AND

c. There is NO opposing traffic.

Any overtaking near junctions must have these considerations whether diagonal stripes exist or not.

These areas are ideal opportunities for frustrated car drivers to overtake with little effort or consideration. You must anticipate this in your riding plan and be prepared to take positive action.

Using a junction to overtake

Overtaking at or near junctions is only dangerous when you do not have all available information and make use of it accordingly, as in the S.T.U.D.D. principle.

Right turns:

When turning from a major to minor road and following another vehicle, good observation and planning can often lead to an overtake immediately upon entering the minor road.

- Your turning arc will have to be smaller, meaning a slower initial speed.
- The machine will be upright sooner than normal.
- A bike's better acceleration can be used to good effect here.
- One gear higher than normal could also be useful.

The same applies when turning from a minor to major road.

- Your turning arc will begin earlier. (See Positioning - Compliance with junction markings page 20.)
- You will move into an empty stretch of road.
- Your superior acceleration completes the manoeuvre.
- One gear higher than normal could also be useful.

Left turns:

Occasions to overtake at left turns are extremely rare as views of traffic and road surface occur very late or even after the turn is completed.

Turning traffic ahead:

Where you are third in a line of vehicles and the lead one is about to turn left or right into a minor road, adjust position, speed and gear to prepare for any overtake which may become possible when the turning vehicle clears. Your anticipation and superior acceleration make it possible. Beware of the vehicle ahead swerving around the turning one and ensure it cannot turn also.

Parking

Where to park

You always want to return to your bike and find it in the same position you left it.

To assist this try to park on a good, firm, level surface where it is on prominent display, yet unobstructive.

Choose a suitable surface.
- Tarmacadam becomes soft in the heat.
- Gravel can move and settle after the stand is set down.
- Oil contaminated areas may not be soft initially but could quickly become so.
- A machine on a side stand has its weight distributed between three points on the ground, a centre stand provides only two. Placing an object such as a squashed can under the side stand foot can be useful to spread the load.

Choose a level surface.
- If not available, one which leans slightly to the machine's left can normally be coped with.
- One leaning to the right should be avoided:
    There is no centre stand lug to help prevent toppling.
    You dismount on the left which is the uphill side and gravity will pull the machine away from you.
- If parking on a gradient is the only option:
    Park facing uphill, it prevents rolling forward off the stand should the machine be caught by a gust of wind or clumsy pedestrian.
    Leave it in gear to prevent movement in either direction.
    A heavily loaded machine on a centre stand may be impossible to get off the stand single-handed, the side stand may be the better option.

On and off the stand

Not all machines are fitted with centre stands.

Those that are vary tremendously in their ease of operation, some being so difficult or unbalancing they should be avoided unless assistance is close by.
- Throwing the machine onto the centre stand after a particularly frustrating journey does no good for anyone, so avoid doing it.
- When you ride a different machine from normal you should check the location and operation of the controls, treat the centre stand the same.

Taking a machine off the stand can be an unnerving experience with some machines. Practice builds confidence.
- Do not put unnecessary weight on the machine by sitting astride and rocking it forward.
- Have a means of stopping it immediately to hand, use the brake lever or, if left in gear the clutch lever.

Check your bike

Start with the obvious and once satisfied each item is OK move on to the next.

All these are simple, take a little time and ensure you do not miss anything which is obviously wrong. Regular weekly and monthly checks for specific readings or pressures are in addition to these.
- As you approach, look at and around the bike. Is anything obviously wrong, flat tyre, leaning to one side, security lock moved or broken, pool of fluid on the floor? Investigate this first.
- Unlock all security devices, especially the steering. Stow locks away.
- Key into the ignition, but do not switch on.

- Check:

    Controls and levels.

    Oil, water, brake fluid, fuel. Turn fuel on
    if necessary.

    Tyre treads for wear, foreign objects
    and cracks.

    Tubed tyres, check valve angle for any
    tyre creep.

    Ignition on, check lights, then switch
    ignition off.

    Brake pressure and clutch free play.

    Any accessories or parts that may have
    become loose.

- Take machine off the stand.
- If it needs manoeuvring backwards
  do it now.
- Sit astride and switch ignition on, checking
  warning lights.
- Start engine and check relevant lights go off.
- If all sounds and feels well move off.
- Within a few yards apply both brakes to
  check for smooth and efficient operation.
- If riding a machine new to you, check the
  response from all controls when fully applied
  as soon as practical, especially the brakes.
- Enjoy the ride.

Things You Didnt Know You Didnt Know

Question

Why do motorcyclists get dazzled more than car drivers?

Answer

On the approach to hill brows motorists wait for the last second before dipping headlights. The last minute is when the opposing headlight appears.

A motorcyclist's riding height is well above headlamp height and you see the oncoming lights before the other driver sees yours, so there will always be that slight delay. Lorry drivers suffer even more!

Question

Why are the headlights of all vehicles on the opposite carriageway of a motorway masked by the central armco barrier?

Answer

Headlights on ALL motor vehicles have to be fitted within defined maximum and minimum heights. Armco is installed at a height designed to restrain vehicles, and appears to coincide with headlamp height.

Question

If the vehicle in front should suddenly stop, what following distance will still result in a collision, no matter how good you or your bike are?

Answer

Courtesy of Len Wayman, Accident Investigator, M.I.T.A.I., M.I.M.I., M.B.A.E.

Car suddenly brakes at 60mph. Takes 4 seconds to come to stop, braking at maximum 0.68g (same as Highway Code). Following motorcyclist reacts to car braking in 0.68 seconds, (Same as Highway Code reaction), but brakes at 0.5g (about as much as a motorcyclist dare risk without lock up of wheels). Motorcyclist takes 5.467 seconds in braking and 0.68 seconds in reaction, total time to react and stop 6.147 seconds. Motorcyclist needs to be at least 57 metres rearward of the car as it brakes if the bike is to stop without hitting the car.

Take this a little further, so that:
The rider has Formula One driver reactions of 0.4 seconds. The rider applies the brakes as above, producing 0.5g. The bike MUST be 30 metres behind to avoid a collision.

Take it to the ultimate, so that:
The rider has Formula One Racing Driver reactions of 0.4 seconds. He can brake to produce 0.68g, the same as a car. The braking distance for both will be the same. The bike MUST be at least 10.7 metres (3 car lengths) behind any vehicle at 60mph - otherwise a collision is inevitable. If you think you can react in 0.4 seconds and brake at 0.68g, good luck.

(At 0.68 seconds reaction time, any closer than 16.6 metres means a collision with no chance of even reaching the brakes! At 0.4 seconds the same will happen if you are closer than 10.2 metres.) (Courtesy of Mike Fell M.I.T.A.I.)

Be sensible - give yourself time to react.

Question

Why does my machine slow down when I ride around a bend?

Answer

Friction. When travelling in a straight line there is a limited amount of friction between the tyre/road interface. If the same amount of power is applied and the machine is 'steered' into a curved path the friction increases and the machine will slow down unless more power is applied to compensate.

A motorcycle can only be 'steered' by turning the handlebars at very low speeds, once a speed is reached where that cannot be done the bike is banked over and handlebar pressure is applied against the toppling from the upright to maintain balance, (counter steering). You can see that the greater 'turning' forces being applied result in the more power required to maintain a given speed.

The reverse applies when the machine returns to upright from a curved path.

(This is the only time I mention counter steering. Although it is a naturally occurring phenomenon I believe that if you have to spend time thinking about it there is something more fundamental wrong with your riding. After all it occurred when you rode your first bicycle and nobody bothered about it then. It did not make you a better cyclist either.)

Roundabout sign

(See illustration at bottom of page 36.)

Answer

The sign is on a dual carriageway. There are warning signs of 'dual carriageway ends' but the primary route sign only shows one road at the 6 o'clock position.

Continental Riding

This chapter has been written by a respected motorcycling friend and one of only two civilian personnel I know in the UK with a Class 1 police advanced motorcycling certificate. He has been an examiner for the IAM since 1991.

Every time I ride on the continent I learn something else which improves my understanding of the way they behave. I try and remember these points for the next time, as they increase my enjoyment or ease problems that arise. I have France in mind for the majority of these points but many equally apply to other countries. I have thought for some time about writing them down, if only to assist my memory. You might have some of your own.

Ferries

- When you pack for your journey, keep things you will want on the ferry, such as toothbrush etc, in one bag so that you can board easily.
- Most companies get you to put your helmet on when riding to the ship.
- The ramp and decks of the ferry can often be wet and slippery.
- The deck hands will tie your bike securely. If they do a really good job, take sea sickness tablets. If you park on the main stand a strap round this and the front wheel gives extra stability.
- If you return to your bike to find it damaged, get the deck officer to agree the damage and make a note of his name. Take a photograph of the damage if appropriate.

General

People will treat motorcyclists as if they were normal human beings, unlike the UK. It helps enormously if you have a dozen words in their language to begin with, such as please, thank you and sorry. They will then speak to you in perfect English.

On the continent they drive on the right. I know that and you know that but you will most likely forget at some point. That point will usually be after you have stopped for a rest, fuel or first thing in the morning. Just when you have it sorted it's time to come home. In the UK we drive on the left...(see above).

The French 'Prioritè á Droite', meaning the vehicle on your right has priority, has been done away with. However not all French people got the memo so watch out. People still fall back on this at tricky junctions in towns, so it's worth remembering.

For all that's said about French drivers they are very positive when they do something. If they pull out in front of you on the autoroute they will get a move on. They don't pull out and then slow down or slow down and then pull out like at home. It's a waste of time trying to let them out because they won't understand. While you need to ride defensively, being as decisive as they are is the best policy. They rarely stop at pedestrian crossings and will probably overtake if you do. Incidentally, the white paint on zebra crossings is especially slippery in the wet, so arrange to ride over the black bit which is plain road surface.

Speeds in general are higher, perhaps because there is less traffic. In smaller towns and villages there might not be a speed limit sign but the 50kph limit begins at the sign with a red border, which shows the name of the place and it ends with the same sign with a line through it. There appears to be an unofficial 70kph-ish limit on the outskirts of these places, which are often straight wide roads. This reduces to 50kph as you get into the town proper and roads become narrower, bendy or populated.

Most motorcyclists wave to each other. The outstretched left arm with 2 fingers is customary and is said to originate because of the battle of Agincourt. The English victors cut off the fingers of the French archers so those that kept their freedom show they still have their fingers. They say!

People you have overtaken are 'waved' to using the right foot.

Signposting

- It helps to have a rough idea of where the major cities are. These are often sign-posted from hundreds of miles away. They choose ones that are just off the bit of map you can see on your tank bag. When you plan your trip note the next major town and the next village on your route plan.
- In general ignore diversion signs which try and send you miles out of your way. You can often get through on a motorcycle. Even when you cannot, there is usually only a short detour round some houses.
- On autoroutes you will notice that destinations in the same direction are on separate signs from those in a different direction. As you approach major junctions and spot your destination, remember the other towns on the same sign. They will omit the town you are looking for from the next signpost but one of the others will be there.
- Also on autoroutes they very helpfully tell you the distance to the next fuel station on the approach to services. However, read the sign carefully because it might say 'vers Lyon' for instance. Which is fine if you are going in the direction of Lyon but chances are you will want the junction 1 mile before the fuel station that goes in a different direction and has no fuel for 20 miles.

Autoroutes

On the approach to toll booths, in general keep to the right where they are manned. Watch for specific motorcycle signs. Some prohibit, some direct. Some bridges are free and they have a narrow motorcycle lane. On some motorcycle race weekends bikes are free.

Be very careful if you see a clear booth at the last minute because someone behind you probably saw it before you. They will be doing a Formula 1 style pit stop.

At some autoroute barriers all you need to do is take a ticket, this often appears automatically, if not push the button. Be aware of the repeater dispenser and button for lorry drivers above your head. They have been known to activate for motorcyclists.

If you are riding in a group it is often quicker for the first bike to pay for everyone. He/she will need the tickets for the entire group so pull alongside and pass them over. When the barrier goes up only one bike should go through. Wait for the barrier to go down and up again before the next bike goes. Pull away from the barrier and off the sensor, or it won't go down. If you are going to wait for your mates you can pull over to the side, but again watch out for cars leaving the booths, the telecart guys don't even have to stop.

If paying by cash, it helps to keep your coins in a small bag or an empty camera film container. As motorcycle tolls are not that expensive you can often just hand the container to the cashiers who will help themselves. That way you don't need to take your gloves off or work out the various denominations of coins.

I'm told that it's a myth that the police time you between stations using your ticket. What actually happens is they set their speed check just before the toll booths, knowing that you will be stopping anyway, so slow down when you see the péage signs.

Should you find yourself out of fuel at a 24 hour credit card only station, most locals will let you use their pump for the reimbursement in cash. UK credit cards don't work in these places yet.

Motorcycle exemptions

There are a number of situations where motorcycles seem to be exempt:

- Parking on paved areas is OK.
- Filtering is expected, except in Germany where it is verboten.
- Overtaking is expected. Cars and trucks in particular will drive up the bank to let you past. It is often better to pass even though you didn't intend to, otherwise sit well back. If you are going faster then them, they will get out of the way. If they are going faster than you, then get out their way.
- If you don't actually stop at a stop sign, don't hang around as someone in a big blue van might be watching.
- The same applies to crossing solid white lines. The French seem to expect it but again don't hang around. They are quite good at warning of a police presence by flashing headlamps.
- If you do get stopped don't try and joke with the officer. Be courteous and show lots of documents, including your registration document. Always carry your documents with you when you are on the bike, even if you are just out for a short ride from your base.
- If there are roads blocked to traffic in protest, such as by lorry drivers, they don't mean motorcyclists.

Conclusion

I hope you have found these guidelines useful and informative.

I have boldly put into print aspects of motorcycling that work for me, but they may not meet with full approval from others. With this in mind I have put forward reasons why things should or should not be done where clarification may be required. All activities and manoeuvres suggested throughout this book must be at your own risk.

Training to develop your skills is available nationwide and should be sought if anything is not clear or appears unsafe.

If you do nothing else with your riding, a saying from the **West Midlands Police Driving School** should always be considered:

Before you do something

Is it safe?
Is it legal?
Is it necessary?

If you like this book and find the information based on my experience useful, tell others. If you find this guidance does not fit in with your own experience or the situations you have to cope with, tell me. Safe riding.

Dave Jones

Index

Notes

Ghosts of Settle-Carlisle Railway

ABOVE: "CITY OF WELLS" IN THE EVENING SUNLIGHT AT RIBBLEHEAD. BELOW: "THE DUCHESS OF HAMILTON" AT BLEA MOOR: AN EXPERIMENTAL PHOTOGRAPH DONE BY REVERSAL PRINTING.

Ghosts of the Settle-Carlisle Railway

**Compiled by
W. R. Mitchell**

**Visuals:
Peter Fox**

Jim Taylor (pictured above) was the stationmaster at Settle in the days when such an official had an imposing cap, with ''scrambled egg'' on the brim. Jim's mind was full of Settle-Carlisle lore. He was fond of telling of the flying sheep. A farmer hurled a dead sheep over a wall on to the track. A passing railway ganger, with more than average strength, promptly hurled it back again! The photograph below is an experimental print from a negative of *Evening Star* climbing towards Aisgill.

GHOSTS?
But shush.....
what was that?

CARLISLE
Corby Castle

Great &
Little Salkelds

Kirkby Thore
Crackenthorpe

APPLEBY
Crosby Garrett
Kirkby Stephen

Mallerstang
Ais Gill

Ribblehead
Salt Lake
Selside
Horton-in
     Ribblesdale
Stainforth
Langcliffe
SETTLE
Settle Junction

Peter Fox   MAP NOT TO SCALE

Typeset and printed by J.W. Lambert & Sons, Station Road, Settle, North Yorkshire, BD24 9AA.
Published by W.R. Mitchell, 18 Yealand Avenue, Giggleswick, Settle, North Yorkshire, BD24 0AY.
© W.R. Mitchell
ISBN 1 871064 11 2

Contents

Illustrations

Front cover: George Horner *(W.R. Mitchell)*. Big John of Selside *(Peter Fox)*. Blea Moor, with signal box and one of the former cottages *(W.R. Mitchell)*. Back cover: *City of Wells* passing Horton-in-Ribblesdale box *(Peter Fox)*. The original layout at Dent. Notice the trackwork, the small shunting yard, the Midland signalbox and two gantry signals *(W.R. Mitchell)*.

This page, above: Reflections on Arten Gill, using a car mirror *(Peter Fox)*.

George Horner: 1. (A photogram of the Ghost of Blea Moor Tunnel).

W.R. Mitchell: 3 (top), 6, 9, 10 (bottom), 13, 20, 22, 23, 26, 35, 36 (top), 37, 39, 42, 43, 45, 46 (bottom, left).

Peter Fox: 7, 10 (top), 12, 21, 24-5, 31, 32, 38, 41 (top), 46 (top), 47.

Drawings and Map by Peter Fox.
Trevor Croucher: 16.

Rowland Lindup: Sketches of workmen.

Bob Swallow: Small maps.

F.S. Williams: Engraving on p.48, of Eden Gorge, from his ''Midland Railway''.

Foreword...
by George Horner
(who was signalman at the remote Blea Moor box)

I ONCE saw a ghost. It was a figure, moving ahead of me as I went on duty at Selside. I'd walked from Horton, in fresh snow. I left a line of tracks. This chap moving ahead of me when I got near the Selside box crossed the tracks. He didn't leave a single footprint!

I've had plenty of chances to see ghosts. For years, Dad and I were among the signalmen who worked shifts at Blea Moor box. Father went up on his push bike from Salt Lake, where we lived at the time. I had a bike at first, then got a lile van. If it was sometimes too wild, we'd walk.

Once, there were folk living up there, to the south of Blea Moor tunnel. They left in the 1960s. After that, being a signalman there was a solitary job. I was often by myself, but never lonely.

I'm glad I'm not the nervous type. In winds, the old box cracked and creaked. If I heard the steps creaking, I'd no idea who it might be. I entertained Bishop Treacy to cups of tea. And I once produced a ghost for a couple of walkers who were wandering about lost. They were off like the wind...

I hope you enjoy these ghost stories about our favourite line. I leave it to you to decide whether or not such things as ghosts exist.

Ghosts? Nay. I've heard nowt you could hang a tale on ....

A BLACK 5 (5407) AT HORTON-IN-RIBBLESDALE.

THE RETIRED railway signalman who spoke these words had been accustomed to "travelling about at all ends o' t'day and neet. It never worried me." He paused to tell me about the time he was cycling home in the gloaming when he saw a strange object on a wall. He heard a cough and the rattling of chains.

The old railwayman laughed at the recollection. "I'd notice a big capstone. And over t'wall a couple of old tups were chained together—horn to horn—so they couldn't fight each other. I'd heard one of 'em cough!"

A ninety-year-old man who was once a ganger at Ribblehead told me of his belief in ghosts. He was not referring to "things"

moving about dressed in large white sheets, but to "chilly presences." When he lived in a railway cottage, a ghost had joined one of the family in bed.

In the old steam-hauled days, smoke from the engine wafted like a ghostly wraith across the carriage window and the drumming of train on the tracks was almost strong enough to change the pattern of the human heartbeat.

The number of ghosts associated with the Settle-Carlisle railway is not large enough to fill a book of this size, so I have added accounts of strange happenings. Some of the most entertaining ghost stories originated in the imagination of the "old hands" on the

7

railway who were trying to scare new-comers. A young signalman posted to a remote box was soon being told about the local ghosts, from a spectral dog to a headless man. A favourite story concerned a man who, decapitated by a passing train, was destined to spend the rest of eternity wandering up and down the track looking for his head.

The truly remote signal boxes, such as Blea Moor or Mallerstang, were spooky places to the most imaginative of men. Long summer days were tolerable. When the long Pennine winter set in, with winds howling like demons, or snow muffling the sound of a human footfall, the slightest creak could make the sensitive signalman's hair rise on the back of his head.

The agony was prolonged by chain-rattling. Dick Clarke, who for many years served in the signal box at Helwith Bridge, was startled by the sound of a chain. When he plucked up courage to wander out of the box, he found it was a collie dog that had broken away from its kennel. The chain had

caught between two capstones as it leapt a wall and the dog was striving vigorously to free itself.

An example of the chain-rattling type of ghost was told to me by signalman Dick Fawcett. This ghost always walked with his back to the trains which, as Dick said, was a dangerous thing to do, even for a ghost. "He was never seen to walk on the 'down' line. How he got back to his starting point, I wouldn't know."

Winter's nights were full of natural sounds—the scream of the white owl questing for voles, the yap of a dog fox on a January night and, as spring approached, the strange bleating sound made by the common snipe as, diving through the still air at daybreak, it extended the stiff outer feathers of its tail. As the wind strummed the barbs, an eerie noise was made.

Dick Fawcett kept a shotgun in the box and had the company of his terrier dog. Taking a dog to work was against Company rules but was tolerated by his immediate superiors. They knew about the remoteness of the box. (Dick was at the time at Eldroth, on the neighbouring *Little North Western* line).

I had many a chat with Dick, who was nicknamed "Rabbity Dick" because of his skill as a poacher. He confirmed that some remote boxes could "get a man down" and "almost send him loony". Men reared in Settle-Carlisle country were less inclined to believe in ghosts than were the young men from town. These men were accustomed to street lighting. They did tend to jump at strange sounds, having seen far too many horror films at the cinema!

In wartime, when not a glimmer of artificial light was allowed, Dick left the signal box with his shotgun on seeing some human forms against the sky. The "strange beings" were members of the local Home Guard. In the same period, men guarding Ribblehead Viaduct in dark or misty conditions were known to challenge a horse or to equate the rustling of a sheep with a German parachutist.

Among the fictional ghosts was that of a railwayman who had been decapitated at a level crossing. His head was never found. "He went out and about looking for it."

Dick Fawcett, who had heard the story, theorised that the head might have been caught up in the motions of the locomotive that struck down the man. "A fitter at Holbeck shed once told me he found a man's hand on a ledge, hidden behind a spring. . ."

Newcomers to a permanent way gang were soon being introduced to the local ghosts and were sent on silly missions. A ganger at Ribblehead had a shock when he saw a new member of the gang running towards Blea Moor, with carpet slippers on his feet. Breathlessly he said he must "stop t'express". One of the gang had been teasing him. He had even gone to the hut and loaned the lad some slippers so that he could run faster!

Ghosts were at their most convincing when firelight or paraffin lamps sent fingers of light into dark places. In the period of full electric lighting and central heating, our homes lack the old sense of mystery. Today, the traditional ghosts, with their white sheets and moaning sounds, are part of the entertainment industry.

Ghosts do not exist, of course.

But, hush — what was that?

St. Leonard's, Chapel-le-Dale, where over 200 railway workers, wives and children were interred in the 1870s.

Above: A Black 5 that has stopped at Settle Junction. *Bottom:* Settle station goods yard as it used to be. Notice the extensive track layout, including the track curving into the goods yard. In close company are the Midland goods shed and the Midland signal box. A water column stands to the left and there are oil lamps on the platform.

The Man in Brown

THE RAILWAY cuts the old town of Settle into two. Midland men reared bridges and gigantic earthen banks across the old market town, severing the opulent *Ashfield Hotel* from the lodge at the end of what had been a drive and emulating the turnpike trustees of the previous century when they claimed a tract of the big garden at Whitefriars.

No ghosts have been reported from the station, though on a winter evening in pre-electricity days the conditions provided an excellent setting for a haunting.

Having joined a committee chaired by the stationmaster, Jim Taylor, I spent many an hour sitting on one of the Bob Cratchitt type stools in the stationmaster's office listening to the affairs in hand—and to the hiss of the paraffin lamp. Shadows contributed to the sense of mystery.

After the meeting, I would begin my homeward walk under the flickering oil lamps, pausing to watch the passage of a steam-hauled train—a ponderous engine, attended by billowing smoke and the prolonged clattering of wagons.

There was a distinctly ghostly feeling in centenary year, 1976, when a special train stopped at Settle and its passengers walked into a marquee set up in the Station Yard. Here a celebratory meal was being served. Some of the carriages had come from the National Railway Museum at York. As they stood in pools of artificial light, waiting for the celebrants to return, they looked like part of a film set—a spy thriller, perhaps.

Settle has its Man in Brown; he belongs to an earlier age than the train, being presumably a monk. Several people have reported seeing a monk-like figure crossing the road at the top of Constitution Hill.

Is this the ghost of Town Head, a mini-mansion that was demolished? On the site of Town Head are some modern bungalows. Bill Jackman, for many years a hairdresser at Settle, was fond of talking about "the Town Head ghost". He was not sure if it was a monk or a vicar!

The oldest folk in Settle remember when Town Head was the home of Dr. Edgar, whose coachman—Mr. Tomlinson—lived just across the road, on the edge of Castleberg. The last occupants were Tot Lord who is remembered as an antiquary and as the founder of the Pig Yard Club. Tot roused the echoes of distant times with his excavations in local caves which had been used by man.

Tot was a down-to-earth character: he was not especially sensitive towards ghosts. As an avid cinema-goer, and patron of the *Nuvic,* he liked a good horror film!

A romantic notion about Buckhaw Brow, the old turnpike route under Giggleswick Scar, claims that horses ''bucked'' as their delicate senses detected lingering traces of the primeval animals whose bones had lain in local caves!

Jack Towler told me that in his youth, 70 years ago, he and David Johnstone, from Selside, visited Settle every Saturday evening. They usually had a drink at the *Golden Lion* before going to the ''pictures'' at the Victoria Hall.

Late one evening, they decided to walk to Langcliffe. As they strolled near ''Brassington's mill'' a chilly ''something'' brought them to a standstill. ''We stopped suddenly—just like a cart jamming up! My mate says: 'What's up?' I said: 'It must be a ghost.' So I don't laugh when anyone mentions ghosts.''

The ghost of a man who hanged himself from a large tree near the railway bridge between Settle and Langcliffe has been reported from this stretch of road. The tree was felled a few years ago as part of a road improvement.

Thirty years ago, two girls who had been dancing were walking on Bond Lane, which flanks the Settle-Carlisle. It was dark; they were holding hands. Both became aware of a ghostly presence; it actually passed between them.

A Black 5 at Settle Junction awaits departure to Carlisle. A photograph taken in April, 1989.

The Rattling Wires

SETTLE JUNCTION, where the Settle-Carlisle breaks away from "the Morecambe line", used to have its own station. Now all that remains is the signal box, which is manned continually. One wild winter night, the signalman had the company of a platelayer connected with some engineering work in the area. At about 2 a.m., the signal wires began to rattle inexplicably.

The platelayer was available to investigate. We went out into the frosty night. The wire had ceased to rattle, which meant that bells in the signal box were silent again. Instead, there was a slurring sound, as though someone was pulling a body along the side of the tracks.

It was not a "someone" but a sheep! This animal had leapt the wall from a field and, on its descent of the bank towards the track-bed, which it doubtless knew from experience was a shade warmer than a field, it had collected some thorny bramble stems which had become firmly attached to the sheep's fleece.

In its progress, the sheep had drawn the brambles over the signal wires and they were now slurring along the ground.

A man with many years of service at Settle Junction box recalled the effect of a thunderstorm on this isolated building. Lightning hit the overhead wire and ran along it to the telephone. The signalman, sitting near the telephone, saw a blue flash extended from the instrument, "You know how lightning is—whoosh, it's gone. That flash did a dance all the way along the lever tops . . . Just for a minute, I didn't feel like picking the telephone up!"

The driver of a steam-hauled train stopped at Settle Junction, reported that he had felt a bump and wondered if he had run over someone. The signalman shone a torch under the locomotive and saw a large tuft of wiry grey hair. "It was bad to see. I was using a lamp under a locomotive at night. The driver daren't touch the stuff!"

A locomotive sent out from Carnforth to Settle Junction could find no body on the track. The hair, sent for analysis, was found to be from a deer.

Much more grim was the discovery by a ganger of a tuft of hair. He saw it by the track and presumed it to be the remains of a rabbit. Turning it over, he saw a human face. And further along the track lay the body of a man who, plainly, had intended to take his own life.

Woman in a Long Gown

THE CONSTRUCTION of the Settle-Carlisle railway had a major impact on the Langcliffe Hall estate. At one time, it seemed that the farmhouse of Barrel Sykes would have to be demolished. In fact, the rails now pass within a few yards of the building.

The Midland company went through the usual legal processes to acquire a strip of land from the estate, which in the 1860s was presided over by Mrs. Jane Perfect.

The family who built Langcliffe Hall in 1602—which is the date carved in stone above the door—is said to have gone bankrupt in the process. The Hall was sold to the Dawsons of Halton Gill, Littondale, in about 1610. Isaac Newton reputedly visited the hall (and, of course, he watched apples fall from the trees in the orchard!). There is no written proof of this.

George Geoffrey Robinson (born 1874), who inherited the estate and changed his name from Robinson to Dawson, was the Geoffrey Dawson who for many years edited *The Times.*

A lofty wall separates the grounds of Langcliffe Hall from the highway. Just across the road is Bowerley, a large house in its own grounds. Several people have testified to the presence of a woman "in an old-fashioned, ankle length dress", crossing the road between the two places. The apparition has been seen to go towards a small gate set in the wall of Langcliffe Hall.

The Hall itself is said to have a female ghost, though she has not been known to cause any trouble.

A Horton man who was courting a lass from Settle some 45 years ago recalls that he was aware of the ghost story as he pedalled his bike up the brow between the Hall and Bowerley after dark, "If there was the slightest unusual sound, I'd pedal like mad!"

The brown lady has not been active in recent times.

The ghost of Christopher Wright, who died in "railway time" (January, 1871), is said to haunt a former beerhouse in West View, Langcliffe. The local name for the small drinking place was the "Pig and Whistle". Wright, the beerhouse-keeper, died at the hands of Ellis Parker, alias Nelson, who had spent nothing but had benefited from a custom known to the navvies whereby one bought a quantity of ale and the others drank indiscriminately, pouring ale into a smaller glass. At closing time on January 15, Ellis Parker refused to leave; he and his mate Tom entered the house-part and in due course Parker struck blows which led to Wright's death. Parker was apprehended and charged with manslaughter; the outcome of his trial is not known. Ghost talk is somewhat vague.

SETTLE TO CARLISLE.

PLAN OF PROPERTY

SITUATE IN THE PARISH OF

Giggleswick

Townships of Settle and Langcliffe

in the

West Riding of the

County of York

belonging to

Mrs Jane Perfect

Shewing the Quantity of Land required
for the purposes of the Railway.

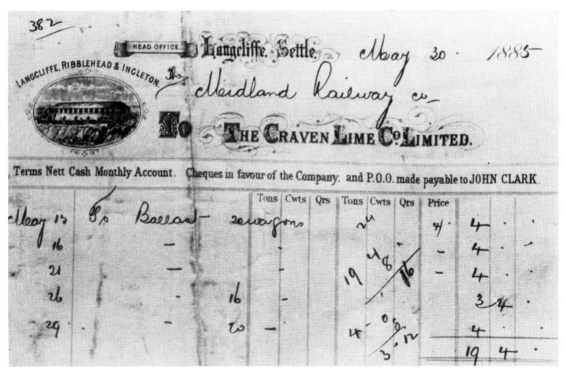

382

HEAD OFFICE — Langcliffe, Settle — May 30 · 1885

LANGCLIFFE, RIBBLEHEAD & INGLETON

Midland Railway Co

To THE CRAVEN LIME Co. LIMITED.

Terms Nett Cash Monthly Account. Cheques in favour of the Company. and P.O.O. made payable to JOHN CLARK.

Date				Tons	Cwts	Qrs	Tons	Cwts	Qrs	Price	
May 13	P.	Ballast	20 wagons				2	4		4	
16	—									4	
21	—			19	8	16				4	
26	—		16							3 4	
29	—		10	—		4	0 12			4	
							3 12			19 4	

The Fickle Chimney

Opposite page: Part of the documentation when the Midland compulsorily purchased for the Settle-Carlisle land belonging to Langcliffe Hall. Above: This account issued by the Craven Lime Company features a drawing of a Hoffman kiln—minus chimney.

LIMESTONE was being transported from Craven Quarry, between Langcliffe and Stainforth, before the Settle-Carlisle line was open throughout. With the lines laid in the south, trains bearing lime could make deliveries to many customers and thus repay the Midland at an early date for the massive expenditure over the new railway.

In 1873, a visitor to Craven Quarry noticed intense activity. Near Willy Wood, houses once occupied by the operatives at the once flourishing but now useless paper mill, the quarrying company was erecting extensive lime works on the patent of Mr. Hoffman.

The Hoffman kiln, for continuous burning of limestone, demanded a large chimney, and in the summer of 1873, this had reached half its total height, which would be 204 feet. "As such a lofty brick structure needed a good foundation, it is built on chisled limestone six feet below the surface. Mr. George Dowson, of Leeds, is the contractor for the chimney, which will take about 200,000 bricks."

For many years, the chimney, with its date of construction picked out in white bricks, was a dominant feature of the upper dale. It was then decided to demolish it. Steeplejacks were brought in. They weakened the structure in the traditional way. It was resolved to contact the BBC so that a television film crew could be in attendance when this massive chimney fell.

On the appointed day, thick mist hung about the valley. The film crew's visit was called off. The workmen went off to the canteen of the paper mill for their breakfast. They returned—to find that the massive chimney had fallen without further human help. There, in the mist, was the county's largest heap of second-hand red bricks.

Had a Ribblesdale boggle given the chimney its final push?

15

WHERE Stainforth Bridge spans the Ribble in a single graceful arch, and the ghost of a man and a dog have been seen, musicians gather to mark the association between that bridge and the composer Edward Elgar.

He visited Ribblesdale on several occasions as the guest of Dr. Charles William Buck of Giggleswick. Buck provided Elgar with a photograph of Stainforth Bridge, which was given a prominent position in his Worcestershire home.

Visible through the arch of the bridge, on the bank of the river, is a mound of stones, now partly grassed over. This marks the site of Robin Hood's Mill, which is said to have been worked on a Sunday and, consequently, aroused the Divine displeasure. The mill sank into the ground, but the grindstones continued to revolve—until some potholers went looking for them and disturbed the conditions which had created the rumbling sound.

The Ghosts of Dog Hill

AFTER passing Craven Quarry, the northward-bound train plunges into a tunnel under the grounds at Taitlands. (During the construction period, the owners of this property were provided with accommodation elsewhere, returning to Taitlands when the noise and bustle of tunnel-excavation was over. Taitlands is now a youth hostel).

Beyond the tunnel is a deep cutting spanned, near the old Stainforth School, by a bridge. This is near Dog Hill. Anyone who crosses the bridge and descends to river level is on Dog Brow.

Stainforth means "stony ford". The ford was no longer necessary when, in the 17th century, Samuel Watson of Knight Stainforth Hall, arranged for the building of the single-span bridge—a most attractive bridge, which since 1931 has belonged to The National Trust.

Almost 40 years have elapsed since Mrs. Maudsley, then the Hall's owner, showed me round her historic home—and told me about the ghosts of man and dog which are said to roam between the Hall and Dog Hill.

She pointed out the hole high on a wall where the ghost is reputed to have lived. How did he get his dog up there? Or was there another hole to serve as a kennel?

Several people in North Ribblesdale claimed to have seen the ghost that regularly exercised his dog. Mrs. Maudsley was not among them. She liked the story!

An early Midland Railway 2-4-0 express engine from the 1870s.

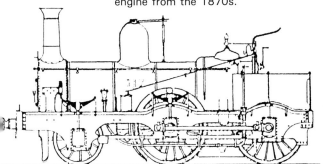

The Silent Bike

AT HORTON, all self-respecting ghosts were deterred by the clamour at the limeworks. The stationmaster had oversight of some busy sidings. The constant clatter of railway wagons would not have given a ghost much peace.

A courting couple, who had been walking towards Selside in autumn, turned back for Horton. As they descended near the road bridge, they saw a man pushing an "old-fashioned" cycle up the road. This was no ordinary bike. Its antiquity was confirmed by the high and solid frame and by the lamp (which emitted a flame and was almost certainly of the carbide variety).

The couple felt they were in the presence of the supernatural when the man pushed the bike by without a sound—no footfalls, no familiar "ticking" sound. The bystanders felt a sudden terrifying chill. And when they turned round to look again—man and bike had vanished.

Had they seen a local ghost known as Big John?

17

An early engine designed by Matthew Kirtley. If the spirit of Matthew endured,
it was surely on the footplate of such a locomotive as this.

Stranger in the Snow

SELSIDE is the hamlet through which motorists drive with care because of the bends in the road. Here the Settle-Carlisle makes its usual purposeful way. The embankment between the railway cottages, to the south, and Selside, features on many photographs taken when steam traction is on the line and the fans are out in their thousands.

A signal box stood here. During the 1939-45 war, it was manned by women. When there was no need for the box, it was carefully dismantled and moved to *Steamtown* at Carnforth.

Selside's railway ghost was seen by George Horner. Early one snowy day, he walked from Horton to Selside to take over his shift at the signal box. The ground was

covered with fresh snow; there was no wind to swirl it around.

George recalls seeing a man moving ahead of him; the man took the path to the box. The stranger's presence did not worry George, for at that time one of the residents of Selside was interested in natural history and he might be seen about at what are now called "unsociable hours".

The figure moving in the snow did not make as though to enter the box but crossed the tracks and vanished from sight. George thought nothing more about it until he realised, with a shock of horror, that—there were no footprints!

A reference has already been made to Big John, the ghost with which many people were familiar. Big John's stay in Selside was seasonal, from October until March. He occupied a decrepit building from which strange tappings were heard, as though John was busy cobbling.

Kit Sedgwick, who lived in the house next door, and had the use of the decrepit premises, worked on the railway but was a cobbler in his spare time. Kit and his wife were familiar with the tapping. When it was heard for the first time in a new season for haunting, one or other of the Sedgwicks would say: "Hello—t'auld lad's landed back."

One night, Kit—having promised to repair a pair of dancing shoes that were urgently required—went to his workroom to finish them. So that villagers would not distract him by calling for a chat, which they were inclined to do—a cobbler's shop being something of a public meeting place—Kit locked the outside door. He finished the shoes and stood looking at them.

Hearing some footsteps on the stairs, he concluded that it was his wife, coming to tell him that supper was ready. He then realised he had locked the door. She could not get in.

Kit left the room as though he had been shot; in "t'middle of t'stairs" he was aware of passing through a chilly area. Reaching

the house, he heard his wife say: "You look as though you've seen a ghost." Kit said: "You shut up—I think I have!"

Kit, still feeling ill at ease, sat down for his supper. As he ate, he heard a ghostly tapping from the upper room. "T'auld lad must have been going to work," said Kit, adding: "And I got in his way!"

As already mentioned, no signalman was keen on being in a box when a thunderstorm was raging. As George Horner says: "Everything buzzes and rattles and rings. Coal in the fire shutters down. It's not a right good experience."

The storm which impressed him most began with a relatively small cloud. "It nobbut looked like a decent-sized football coming across. A black thing. Mind you, there was thunder about and there had been all day. There was one unholy bang and a flash right on t'top o' t'box."

George, sitting on the locker end, heard a bang from a fuse box nearby. He later found it had been affected by lightning and metal pieces had become one solid piece. The fuse box cover lay in bits on the floor, "I thought: 'If thou's getting in, I'm getting out'." He went to the door. Lightning struck the area again—and again. It was a terrifying time.

A Midnight Mishap

ON A WET and windy October in 1968, the Selside signalman was informed by Blea Moor box that the locomotive hauling the Edgehill to Carlisle freight had failed at Blea Moor. He brought the 20-19 (Warrington-Carlisle) freight to a halt at the home signal, just short of the box.

Meanwhile, further down the line, the 22-15 (Preston-Carlisle) freight was coming up the Drag and fast approaching Horton-in-Ribblesdale. With a stationary freight at Selside, the Horton signalman had all his signals at the "on" (stop) position.

The 22-15 approached the Horton box under power. The signalman waved a red hand lamp,

but this too brought no response. He sent a "train running away" bell signal to Selside. The Preston freight, thundering up the 1 in 100 gradient towards Selside, passed the distant signal at caution and, travelling at about 30 mph, collided with the rear of the stationary freight. A derailment occurred.

Clearing the permanent way took two full days. Nearly 200 trains of all kinds were affected by the closure. The clearance of wreckage took several weeks.

At a Ministry of Transport inquiry, it was disclosed that both the driver and second man of the Preston-Carlisle freight had fallen asleep.

Salt Lake Cottages, between Selside and Ribblehead. One Cottage was haunted by a ''chilly presence''.

A Ghost Who Went to Bed

WHEN the Midland built its line from Settle to Carlisle, part of it passed through such thinly-populated countryside that ''railway servants' cottages'' were built for the porters, platelayers and signalmen who would maintain the line.

The best-known of these, because of their solitary position in the Three Peaks Country, are known as Salt Lake Cottages. They stand in all their Victorian gothic splendour between Selside and Ribblehead.

These cottages were well-built, of stone, with steeply-pitched roofs. Each porch was partitioned within, so that it might serve two adjacent cottages. And each cottage was provided with a yard, a wash-house and out-side toilet—luxury indeed for ordinary folk in the 1870s.

Today, the cottages are privately owned. They still belonged to the railway when Mr and Mrs Jack Towler lived at one of them.

Jack, a platelayer, became ganger on the celebrated Ribblehead stretch.

Mrs. Towler's recollections indicate that life at Salt Lake was never dull. She went across the yard to fill the wash-boiler and to light a fire under it for the weekly wash. The farmer from Gauber was driving some cows along the track at the back of the Cottages.

''The cows had just been turned out of the shippons after the winter. One of the cows saw my open back-door and probably thought it was a shippon. As I came out of the wash-house, I saw the cow going into the house, I shouted to the farmer; he followed the cow through two doors into the front room!''

Mr. Cockles, the ganger, had a hen hut in a field just below the Cottages. The Towlers had a stuffed fox which Mrs. Towler wished to dispose of. For a bit of a lark, a friend took it from its glass case at night and set it up in front of the hen hut. A local man, seeing the fox, got his gun, stalked the fox, climbing over the wall, moving down the railside and shooting the fox at close range. "It blew t'auld fox into little bits."

The ghost of No. 1 Salt Lake Cottages did not wear a white sheet, nor did it wail during the night. It most certainly did not go in for the common chain-rattling routine. This ghost was a "chilly presence."

It was discovered that a platelayer who lived there had been killed when struck by a train on the Dent Head length; he left a wife and a son. The hauntings began at the time of the accident. The front bedroom of the house had a special attraction for the ghost, which sometimes crept into bed, scaring the occupant. The first time it happened, the awakened sleeper, feeling this "ghostly presence"—this limited area of intense cold—was unable to move or scream for a while.

Mrs. Towler was aware of the near presence of the ghost when "something" came across her face. "It was just like being stroked with a big feather duster. The ghost had come from the front bedroom into ours."

There was something supernatural— somewhere!

An unusual smoke effect at Ribblehead when Black 5 (5407) was climbing towards Blea Moor. For once, the wind was blowing from the east rather than from the west.

A Class 25 on a mixed freight train of the sort that was seen in the late 1960s. Sadly, there is no more freight on the line. In the foreground of the picture is the Station Hotel.

Lost—and Regained

RIBBLEHEAD VIADUCT is far too wild for a ghost. When a westerly gale is being funnelled by Chapel-le-Dale, it hits the viaduct with astonishing force; the moan of the wind through the arches is like part of the soundtrack of a Brontë film.

A hoary story tells of a railwayman who was walking across the viaduct in such conditions. The wind blew the cap off his head, over the side, through one of the arches and back on to his head. It would have been a better story if the hat had been replaced the right way round!

The story would have been better still if it were true. The parapets of the viaduct are so high that, generally, a westerly gale is

deflected well above the head of a walker on the viaduct.

In the railway construction period, a large pothole—Batty Wife Hole—was filled in because it lay on the route the lines were to take. Who was Mrs. Batty? Some said that she lived in the district. Mr. and Mrs. Batty were always arguing and eventually she walked out on him. He pleaded for a reconciliation, and a meeting was arranged—beside the big pothole, which incidentally has a pool at the bottom.

Mrs. Batty was the first to turn up. She waited for a long time, but no one arrived. So depressed was she that she leapt into the pool and was drowned. When the husband turned up and discovered what had happened, he also took his life in the pool.

A more prosaic explanation of the name Batty Wife Hole is that Mrs. Batty was the wife of a local farmer who used the pool for the weekly wash.

If the Settle-Carlisle was to have a ghost train, it would surely be *Bonnyface,* the Bradford-Hawes express. It was no bonnier that the other great steam locomotives that hauled trains over the Pennines. Blackened by soot, streaked by a Pennine rain shower, and basking in a cloud of steam after the weary miles of the Drag from Settle, its face was not really bonny at all.

Yet for years—and some said it was since the train first ran in 1889—the Bradford-Hawes train was known as Bonnyface.

One explanation is that previously the workmen had to travel in freight vans. An express would be an attractive means of transport after that. Another story told is that the nickname was a skit on a rather ugly permanent way inspector who travelled regularly on this train. The railwaymen said he travelled half-fare because the top part of his body was invariably protruding from the window as he checked their work.

A third story to account for the name Bonnyface is that the train ran about the time the platelayers and quarrymen were ending work for the day. When they saw it pass on its way back to Bradford, they knew it was time for tea!

Over 200 people died at the shanty towns spread across the moor at Ribblehead when the Settle-Carlisle line was being constructed (1869-1876). It is not surprising that several times, especially when there has been sunlit mist, I have felt a spinal chill while following the bed of the former tramway to visit the sites of the shanty towns.

The tendency of a navvy to drink heavily led to many a death. Some men, staggering from the beer-houses, found the driest place for a nap. It so happened that the tramway was driest. Over the years, one or two men who had rested their heads on a rail were decapitated by the first train of the following day.

Some official visitors to Batty Green, the largest of the shanty towns, were shown the hospital and then entered the dead-house [mortuary]. One of the party lifted the lid off a new coffin—and was startled to find it contained a body. Had the authorities forgotten to bury him? Surely not. This body was fully clad.

The lid was lifted again. The man who lay, face-down, in the coffin wore blood-stained clothing! Had he been murdered? The Coroner must be informed.

Another man approached the coffin and, in order to see if the flesh was rigid or flabby, pinched the man's left leg. The "corpse" raised his head and cried out: "Can't you let a poor fellow sleep quietly?"

He had been sleeping off the effects of a night's hard drinking. He was told that, while in a stupor, he might have been buried alive. In any case, that coffin was used for the reception of people who had been suffering from smallpox and fevers.

The navvy asked for thruppence—so that he could get another pint of beer—and he was then heard enquiring the way to Keighley.

Ribblehead Station in its complete state. Since then, the buildings have been much modified and the Stationmaster's House is in private hands.

Black 5 (5407) storming through Garsdale in the early 1980s. The land to the left of the photograph is where, early in the century, a locomotive was said to have rolled down the embankment, to gradually sink into the earth and be lost to sight. People talked of the ghostly loco for many years; then the chimney was located and, in 1989, a serious attempt to locate the whole was mounted, using a metal detector. Only the chimney was found. The ghost proved to be a Victorian spoof. Restored and re-painted, the chimney stood for a time in the waiting room at Appleby station.

Boggle at Hurtle Pot

RIBBLEHEAD lay in the parish of Ingleton Fells. Any funerals involving railway workers were conducted in Chapel-le-Dale, where as the years went by the churchyard had to be extended.

Hurtle Pot, behind the little Chapel, was said to be the haunt of a boggle which lured visitors to their doom in a deep pool (a pool inhabited by "black troutes").

When weird strains were heard by a courting couple passing on the nearby track, they scurried away. Eventually, from Hurtle Pot, a man emerged. He had been practising playing the violin!

BURIALS in the Parish of *Chapelle dale or Ingleton Fells*
in the County of *Yorks* in the Year 18*74*

Name.	Abode.	When buried.	Age.	By whom the Ceremony was performed.
Lewis Roberts No. 401.	Blea-moor in Ingleton Fells	July 19th	32	E. Smith M.A. Vicar
William Dyke No. 402.	Bleamoor Tunnel	Augt 2nd	40	E Smith M.A. Vicar
Sarah, Grace Metcalfe No. 403.	Ingleton	Augt 31.	19 years	E. Smith M.A. Vicar.
Sarah Ann Cameron No. 404.	Batty green	Sept 18.	1 year	E. Smith M.A. Vicar
Richard Wright No. 405.	Batty green	Novbr 16th	25 years	T. Dod Sherlock off: Min:
Robert Hepinstall No. 406.	The Tunnel Huts Ingleton Fells.	Nov. 17th	37 years	T. Dod Sherlock off: Min:
Annie Smith. No. 407.	Chapel le Dale.	Nov. 26th	21 years	T. Dod Sherlock off: Min:

Opposite page: St Leonard's, Chapel-le-Dale and the marble plaque (within the little chapel) which commemorates those who died during the construction of the Settle-Carlisle. *Above:* A page from the burials register kept at St Leonard's in "railway time". Notice the names of shanty towns in the column headed "abode".

Lile Hob Gets a Ride

TO THE MIDLAND MEN, Blea Moor was a fearsome obstruction through which they must tunnel. Several ventilation holes were left. In the Steam Age, Blea Moor was The Smoky Mountain.

James Allport, the Midland general manager, asked by a portrait painter what sort of background he would like, requested an impression of Blea Moor, which had given him so many headaches in the construction period of 1969-76.

Blea Moor, before "railway time", was a tract of heather crossed by the Lancaster-Richmond turnpike and a few old farm tracks. It was at this time that Lile Hob o'Blea Moor was particularly active. This droll little chap was known to rest his feet by jumping on the back of carts being driven on the moor road.

He was a genial hob. The local people were really quite fond of him!

Now the Settle-Carlisle sweeps up from Ribblehead Viaduct and runs some 500 feet below the moor top in a tunnel. Over a century ago, this was excavated by small teams of miners. Some of those who maintained the tunnel were provided with cottages on the south side of the tunnel, in the vicinity of the signal box, which originally stood by the "down" line and is now beside the "up". Blea Moor box is much more modern than the typical Midland type.

This became a remote box in the 1960s, when the cottages were vacated. A tale is told of a railwayman who hanged himself in one of the cottages; the body was discovered when his wife, returning from

Settle, could not get into the house—and, peering through the window, she noticed on the table the undisturbed lunch box she had packed for him that morning.

George Horner, who was a signalman at Blea Moor for many years, recalls when a train was stopped at the box. One of the crew reported "a leet wandering about at tunnel end." It was 11pm. With no imminent traffic, George reported to his colleagues by phone that he intended to investigate the phenomenon.

One o' lads said, when George reported back: "Thou wouldn't have getten me up there at that time o'neet." What the footplate men had seen was a fish-tail lamp where there was a "slack" because of work on the permanent way.

Late one night, "heavy breathing" on the telephone would have upset many people.

George instantly realised that someone had picked up the phone at the north end of the loop and was having a prank.

The tables were turned when two visitors called. As the Good Book has it, "the night was far spent". It was a Saturday night and there was a hush on the Settle-Carlisle line. "Because there were no trains about, I turned down t'light and sat looking into t'fire. I put a vessel out of a handlamp on top of t'book end to give a bit of a glimmer."

The ticking of the clock and an occasional splutter from the fire marked the passing of time. "I was nice and comfortable." Then George heard the sound of footsteps on the steps leading to the door of the box. Here he was, alone at night, a mile or two from the busy world, and there were some unexpected visitors.

George, wondering who could be calling so late at night, went to the door and found two walkers who had been on the fells and were lost. He gave them directions. The two men stood in the box, as though finding some comfort in the warmth.

One said: "Don't you get lonely at a place like this?" George assured him that he was quite happy with his own company. He said that now and again he did get a bit of com-

Men died in Blea Moor tunnel because of their too casual approach to dynamite, which in the 1870s was a comparatively new type of explosive.

pany. "There's a bloke who comes, late on at neet. He comes for a brew. Then he makes his way back to wherever he lives". "Who's he?" queried one of the walkers.

George gravely told him about the accident that led to the death of a local man, and how he could not bear to be away from Blea Moor for long. George added: "I usually expect him on a neet like this—it's a fine neet, but windy—and he always makes plenty o'noise when he comes, though he's quiet enough when he's had his brew."

The visitors shuddered. One asked: "How do you know when he's come?"

"Well," said George, "T'wind blows t'door oppen and this little leet"—he pointed to the flame from the vessel standing on the book—"goes out."

Let George tell the rest of the tale in his own words. "It couldn't have happened better if I'd planned it. They were standing just inside t' door. They must not have shut it properly. And it really was windy. T'door blew oppen and t'little leet went out.

"By gum, I said—THERE HE IS! When I looked round, there wasn't a soul to be

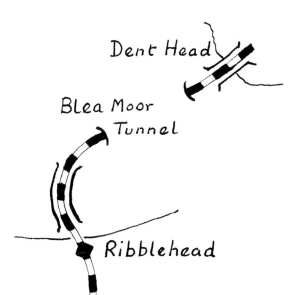

Dent Head

Blea Moor
Tunnel

Ribblehead

seen—just a couple o'leets departing across t'moor. I bet they told a real tale when they got to Ingleton . . . ''

Blea Moor box is a creaky structure in a high wind. It is more modern than many, with larger windows. ''A south-westerly gale beats against those windows, and I've actually seen t'glass move in and out as wind pressure builds up and is released.

''I was telling a bloke on the phone about this. I said t'glass was coming in about an inch. He said: 'Aye, it's terrible wild; I've been hanging on to locker up here.' A few months later he was relieving Blea Moor and I was relieving him. He said: 'I thought it was a cock and bull story, but that glass came in about an inch today. It freetened me to deearth. I kept thinking that any minute now it will break and there'll be glass everywhere.' It never did.''

Workers in Blea Moor Tunnel at the time when 100 steam trains a day were passing through were provided with naptha lamps. The light did not penetrate far in the fug composed of engine smoke. Sometimes a platelayer found his way by tapping a stick against the rails.

Harry Cox, who worked for the Midland before the 1914-18 war, was in Blea Moor in dense smoke as yet another train went by with a clatter and a roar. Now the smoke was so thick, it could almost be chewed. Harry's quick wits recorded a swishing sound from the tunnel side, as though someone had thrown himself from the train.

He prodded with his stick and eventually it encountered something that was large and flabby. A corpse? No—it was an extremely large fish, doubtless jettisoned by a cook on the passing express train.

Tragedies at Blea Moor

STEEL RAILS sweep into Blea Moor. The railway tunnel reaches a depth of 500 feet below the moor's peaty surface. With a length of 2,629 yards, the tunnel took five years to excavate.

A visitor of 1873 noted: ''In the Tunnel, the work never stops from Sunday night at ten, until Saturday night at the same time—relays of men relieving one another at 6am and 6pm. It is formed by hand drilling, filling the holes with gun-cotton or gun-powder, and then igniting by means of a time fuse.

''The debris is then cleared away, either up the shafts in 'skeps' or in waggons at the open end; the brick lining follows as soon as possible.

''The light is obtained by means of tallow candles, and has a pretty effect.''

When it was complete, and traffic was passing through it, there remained the task of maintenance in grim conditions of smoke and soot.

A permanent way inspector, engaged in weighing rails in Blea Moor, took a rubbing of a rail and accidentally slipped backwards as the men canted over the rail, which had been supported by wooden blocks. He was lucky to get away with a bruising. On the other hand, a platelayer working near Blea Moor signal box, to the south of the tunnel, was killed when he was struck by a train.

One April day in 1952, the 9.15am

Ventilation shaft on Blea Moor, with Ingleborough in the distance. The fine mesh on top is designed to stop ''foreign bodies'' such as stones from being lobbed into the shaft and thence to the tunnel, far below.

Thames-Clyde express (Glasgow to St. Pancras) emerged from the southern end of Blea Moor Tunnel at speed only to meet disaster on the facing points of the ''up'' loop, near the signal box.

Compound locomotive A1040, which was piloting the train, remained on the track but A6117 *Welsh Guardsman* was derailed and ploughed into the ballast on her side. The first three of the 10 coaches which made up the train zig-zagged across all four running lines, while the following four coaches were derailed but remained upright.

The train was carrying some 200 passengers. Fortunately, considering the speed at which the train had been travelling, no one was killed. Twenty-nine people, including some railwaymen, were injured.

An inquiry discovered the cause of the accident—bad maintenance on the Compound. The unsatisfactory fitting of a split pin in the tender brake rod mechanism had resulted in the pin shearing off, allowing the adjustable brake rod to come adrift. When the leading engine hit the points, the rod struck the lock stretcher bar and moved the knife edges sufficiently to derail *Welsh Guardsman* and the leading coaches.

As the ambulance team arrived at Blea Moor, the members were horrified to see rows of bodies laid out on the embankment near the signal box. In the circumstances, they presumed that all these people had died. The passengers were simply resting in the sunlight at this desolate spot until help arrived.

Above: A Class 31 locomotive with a service train bursts out of Shotlock Hill tunnel with a dark cloud of exhaust fumes. *Below:* The *Duchess of Hamilton,* newly restored in 1990, on a rising gradient near the cottages at Selside. Telegraph poles are seen to be above ground. Elsewhere, almost all the wires are laid underground. *Opposite page:* From a ganger's book, dated April 1, 1886. The line had been opened to passenger traffic for just 10 years. Note the attractive copperplate hand-writing and the modest return received by a worker. The ganger was paid only 4s.6d a day.

GANGER'S TIME BOOK. Little Barbee BRANCH. E. B. 10.

from 14 m. 20 ch. to 16 m. 10 ch.

For Week ending April 1 1886

Bemrose & Sons, Printers, 23, Old Bailey, London; and Derby.

NAME.	OCCUPATION.	F.	S.	Sun	M.	T.	W.	T.	T.	Total Days	Rate.		REMARKS.
Mason Thomas	Ganger 2/.	1	1		1	1	1	1	1	6	4/6	1 7	Repairing
Fothergill John	under "	1	1		1		1	1	1	6	3/6	1 2	Permanent
Clarke Joseph	Lab. 2/.	1	1		1	2	1	1	1	6	3/4	1	Way
Flack George No 2.	1	1	1		1		1	1	1	6	"	1	"
Stevenson William	"	1	1		1		1	1	1	6	"	1	"
Johnston Andrew	Boy	1	1		1		1	1	1	6	"	1	"
		W. 8										2 9	Pay at Little

April 15 1886

NAME.	OCCUPATION.	F.	S.	Sun	M.	T.	W.	T.	T.	Total Days	Rate.		REMARKS.
Mason Thomas	Ganger 2/.	1	1		1	1	1	1	1	6	4/6	1 7	Repairing
Fothergill John	under "	1	1		1	1	1	1	1	6	3/6	1 2	Permanent
Clarke Joseph	Lab. 2/.	1	1		1	1	1	1	1	6	3/4	1	Way
Flack George No 2.	"	2	2		1	1	1	1	1	5 7	"	18 7	"
Stevenson William	"	1	1		1	1	1	1	1	6	"	1	"
Johnston Andrew	Boy	1	1		1	1	1	1	1	6	"	1	"
												6 7 4	Pay at Little

An Echoing Cavern at Rise Hill

"To a stranger, it has been truly said by one who visited this tunnel, there is something unearthly in the sounds and sights of these mining operations..."
(Williams, The Midland Railway, 1877).

IF THE SPIRITS of long-dead miners frequent Rise Hill, between Dent and Garsdale, they will include a man who, in a fit of depression, while visiting a toilet block situated near the south end of the tunnel, cut his throat.

The Settle-Carlisle is a comparatively modern intrusion in this high fell country. It is an area where place names hint at the sodden nature of the terrain—Black Hill, Black Hill Moss, Blackmire, Dodderham Moss...

A "shanty town" was built near the site of the tunnel. Three hundred people lived up there, 1,300 feet above sea level. The rumbling of wagons, and an occasional scream as an accident occurred, marked the presence of an incline railway that conveyed workers and materials to and from Garsdale.

A tunnel originally known as Black Moss, and subsequently named Rise Hill, was a desolate spot for a major feat of civil engineering. Williams, early in the construction period, toiled up Cow Gill ravine and came to a small opening in the side of the hill. He had reached the temporary heading into the tunnel.

"There is not much to be seen here, so we mount to the top, go as far as the first shaft, and taking our place in the iron 'skep', at a given signal are rapidly lowered in to the depths below."

Williams, after a dizzying descent, waited until his eyes were accustomed to the gloom. He and the others with him gratefully accepted the gift of candles. The party carefully picked its way to where the miners were at work, creating a subterranean passage 26 feet wide and 20 feet high.

"After a long walk, we arrive at the face, where we see some 30 or 40 miners hard at work." He saw traditional activity. A man held a jumper [drill] which was struck by another man using a heavy hammer. Repeated blows drove the jumper into the rock, the hole being then packed with gunpowder and detonated to bring down more rock. In due course, dynamite was being used.

As Williams and his friends were leaving, they heard explosions. The ground shook beneath their feet. "The miners were firing the charges in the pit blow." The miners drove a way through rock, but it was less firm than expected and so most of the tunnel had to be lined, and reinforced with wrought iron ribs, greatly delaying work and increasing the cost.

For years, a visitor to Rise Hill could see slagheaps composed of displaced material lifted up the shafts from the tunnel. Some of these heaps were eventually used for roads, permission having been obtained to plant a new conifer forest here. The modern train leaves the open bleak fell country behind at Dent and enters an area where the dark, drool conifers give a backwoods impression to the scene.

Approach to the Summit Length

Above: A Class 31 thundering through Dent station.
Right: The same train, moments later, as it clears the platforms. In view is the signal box, which has been demolished. The stone bothy was used in times of snow.

Left: Signal box at Garsdale, now infrequently used. Gone is the Garsdale tank house, in which dancing took place in the 1930s.

Ex-Midland 4F (44324) is shown at Aisgill Sidings, awaiting a path to Carlisle. A picture from the 1960s.

Left and below: Dealing with a heavy snowfall at Aisgill in (probably) 1947. The engine appears to have been one from the Scottish Division.

The Ghost who Blinked

THE RAILWAY, having reached its summit at Aisgill, now runs on a ledge cut from the lower slopes of Wild Boar Fell, and offers passengers some lingering views of Mallerstang, the "cradle" of the River Eden. One of the wooden cabins used by the platelayers became known as Hangman's Cabin because a man hanged himself here. He had been feeling very depressed.

Arthur Taylor, of Appleby, looked like a ghost when he emerged blinking from the muddy confines of a local culvert which he and a colleague had been attempting to free when a storm almost blocked it with uprooted trees, mud and other debris.

Arthur remembers the enormous size of the culvert and how he and the man from Kirkby Stephen worked hard to free it and relieve the pressure of flood water on the railway. Their efforts eventually showed signs of success.

As the water began to break through, he climbed part way up a ladder on the low side of the culvert. The dam burst. The pressure of the water forced the ladder—and Mr. Taylor—out, until it was almost horizontal.

He lost sight of the other man, but eventually staggered to the top side of the culvert and found him; they returned home as soon as possible, covered with mud which now was drying, giving them a distinctly ghostlike appearance.

In the valley is Pendragon Castle, with its Arthurian connections. Uther Pendragon, the father of Arthur, is said to have built the

CULVERT TO THE SOUTH OF DENT STATION.

castle (a statement which a historian would immediately dispute). He spent much time trying to divert the river Eden so that it would form a moat. A famous couplet asserts:

*Let Uther Pendragon do what he can
Eden shall run as Eden ran.*

Nicholls, a clergyman/historian of the locality, who mentioned the intense interest shown by local people in passing trains when the railway was newly opened—some went out by night for the spectacle of a glare from the firebox—gave us information about local superstitions.

"There was Rob Roy, who was said to inhabit a cave at Castlethwaite; and the black hen, which invariably frustrated all attempts to unearth the buried treasure—a chest of gold—of Pendragon Castle, by scratching in at night the soil that has been dug out by day.

"Beautiful white ladies, it is said, had been seen walking about the ruins of Pendragon Castle at the witching hour of twelve o'clock at night. Also it was said that a headless ghost had been seen coming out of the gate before the castle. And as an indication that the castle was regarded as the rendezvous of ghosts, I learn that two or three of the fields adjoining it are called 'Boggles'.

"In your dale fifty years ago [i.e., about 1830] when the hearthstone of a Deepdale farmhouse was taken up, the discovery was made of two or three brown earthenware bottles, each bottle being full of crooked pins, which the residents used as a charm to keep off evil spirits."

A signalman who had to travel to his work at Mallerstang by motor cycle told me of the spookiness of night shifts. He would leave his machine in the churchyard at Outhgill and set off "up the hillside", hoping to find the stiles; otherwise, he would have to clamber over the walls and might meet the track well away from the box.

"When the night was dark and the weather was really bad, I'd to wait until the next train came before I knew I was going in the right direction!"

Bahamas, just after its restoration, climbing on a summer's day. The photographic viewpoint is Aisgill bridge. Seen in the background is the bridge sometimes referred to as Hangman's Bridge, after a suicide of long ago.

A MALLERSTANG ACCOMMODATION BRIDGE, VIEWED FROM A CLASS 40.

The Devil's Mill

IN MALLERSTANG, a traveller is not acutely aware of the famous railway, which—after being gloriously in view near Aisgill—plays hide and seek on the western flanks. The old Midland station is beside the road high above the town. The North Eastern system had the prime valley site.

Not far from the old station lies Skenkrith, a spectacular limestone gorge. This includes a feature known as Coup Keinan Holme, where a small stream goes underground. A visitor can, under certain conditions, hear the water rumbling on its subterranean course. The sound has been compared to machinery and the feature itself was called Devil's Mustard Mill.

(The same phenomenon was to be found at a hole just above Stainforth Bridge in Ribblesdale, where the name given was Robin Hood's Mill. Robin was, indeed, a local miller who worked on the Sabbath; the mill sank into the ground but the grindstones continued to revolve).

Jingling Annas, a wandering spirit detected between Winton and Kirkby Stephen, was exorcised near the bridge crossing the Eden. A wise man from Stainmoor spoke the words. The quiescent spirit is said to lie under a large rock.

An old tailor who frequently walked from farm to farm in the same area created his own ghost. The strange sound he heard as he walked back to Kirkby Stephen one moonlit night was the knapping of his own shears and lapboard. The tailor began to run. The "ghost" quickened its pace; the shears calling "catch him?" "catch him!" At least, that's what they seemed to say.

As he got over a stile, and the ghostly chatter ended, he realised with intense relief what had caused the sound.

Building the Church

THE EDEN VALLEY opens out like a fan between the Lake District and Northern Pennines. So broad does the valley become that it is not easy, using the roads, without a good map or local knowledge, to follow the course taken by the Settle-Carlisle.

Crosby Garrett, an obscure little village lying to the west of Kirkby Stephen, had a busy station mainly because of the importance of farming. For example, the milk train called here each evening on its way to the dairy at Appleby.

The station is no more, most of the buildings having been demolished and the platforms becoming weed-strewn.

Crosby Garrett church, which has a prominent site on a knoll, was originally to have been built in the valley. Stone and timber were taken to the site by day. They were mysteriously transported to the top of the hill at night.

Eventually, the villagers took the hint and built their church on the knoll.

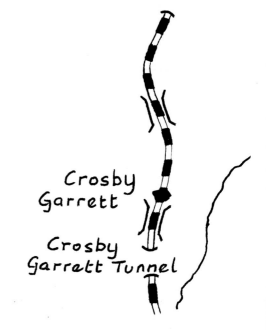

Crosby Garrett

Crosby Garrett Tunnel

A Druid's Stone

MR. CRACKENTHORPE, of Newbiggin Hall, achieved lasting fame in the annals of the Settle-Carlisle as the landowner who, when the Midland engineers proposed to fell the trees in his favourite wood, which was on the route for the new railway, asked if one tree might be spared.

The engineers asked why. He said: "So that I can hang the lot of you on it!"

At the hamlet of Crackenthorpe, near Appleby, they had a gibbet on which to hang the wrongdoers. Their bodies would be a deterrent to other mischief-makers.

Peg Sneddle was said to weep for her lover, who met such a fate, as she drove a carriage—hauled by headless horses!—between the gibbet and an oak on the hill opposite what was to become Kirkby Thore railway station.

The ancient oak was in a place that offered a clear view of Cross Fell. The Druids gathered at Midsummer to witness the rising of the sun. A standing stone in the Druid's field was destroyed by a Mr. Nicholson. He used gunpowder, igniting it when the people—the possible objectors to his plan—were attending a Sunday service in church.

Above: Low House Crossing, which has been modernised. Notice the old type upper quandrant signals, of which few remain on the Settle-Carlisle.
Below: Crosby Garrett, pictured in its heyday. Most of the buildings have been demolished. The station was unusual in that the road bridge springs from the middle of the platforms.

Voices Beneath the Track

ONE SUNDAY, a ganger who was walking his length stopped near Kirkby Thore on hearing the sound of ''something dropping''. He looked round. ''I couldn't see a thing.''

The bemused ganger stood and listened. He then located the source of the noise. Ballast was seeping into the local mine.

He heard miners talking! A ''slack'' was introduced. In due course, the mine workings at this point were reinforced by concrete. Railwaymen have wryly observed of the area of the ''slack'' that here ''the Settle-Carlisle runs on pit props.''

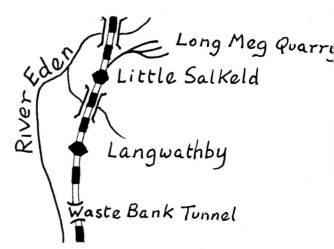

A Matter of Luck

THE LUCK of Burrell Green, an old brass dish, is said to have been given to a local family by a ''being'' called Nob-i-th-hurst and

If e'er this dish be sold or gi'en
Farewell the Luck of Burrell Green.

The Luck of Eden Hall was (it is said) given to a servant who was fetching water from a local well. Inexplicably, he was doing this in the moonlight.

The servant observed some fairies who were dancing on the lawn around what proved to be a glass vessel, green in colour, adorned by red, yellow and blue enamel. The servant decided to relieve the fairies of the responsibility of looking after the goblet. They warned the servant that, should the goblet break or fall, luck would depart from Eden Hall.

A more likely story is that the vessel was brought to the Hall by a member of the landed family who was returning from the Crusades. (The Luck of Eden Hall has been kept in recent years in the Victoria and Albert Museum).

Duchess of Hamilton, hauling a steam special, on a run-past at Appleby.

Storied
Stones

Above: Long Meg.
Below: Her Daughters. The
famous Stone Circle is to be
found near Salkeld. The product of the Long Meg mine
was once cleared by the
Settle-Carlisle, there being
special sidings. A local
farmer heard the "krump" of
explosions as miners worked the night shift.

Red Faces in a Sandstone Gorge

THE EDEN was running high, forcing us to remove our footwear and wade in what hopefully were the shallows, close up to a red sandstone cliff, part of the Eden Gorge.

Above the sound of water came the rapid trill of a sandpiper, the metallic alarm call—zit, zit—of the dipper and a heron's coarse and somewhat doleful cry of annoyance at our intrusion.

From beyond the river came the klaxon call of a diesel-hauled train, part of the regular passenger service. A friend who explored that far bank told me with joy that the only other person he saw all day was a BR driver, in his cab, who returned his wave.

This area where the Eden has made a deep and dramatic bed for itself is craggy, well-wooded and somewhat Scottish in character, with tufts of heather and pines that have an orange glow when the westering sun is upon them. A rail passenger might see an alert roebuck. It is as though the northbound rail traveller is being prepared for an imminent entry into the real Scotland.

We waded further upriver, setting off more calls in the early warning system of bird and beast. Now I heard the gruff bark of a testy old buck. We were intent on reaching a secluded little cove—a cove not visible from the rocks above—where a Cumbrian ecentric, William Mounsey, left an array of carvings on the soft red rock.

With the water lapping against our rolled-up trousers, we rounded a corner— and beheld this mysterious little place where graffiti has attained the quality of art. Mounsey, seeing the sheer redstone walls of Eden Gorge, had been impelled to copy a few lines from Izaac Walton's

Compleat Angler:

> Oh the fisher's gentle life
> Happiest is of any.
> Void of pleasure, full of strife
> And beloved by many.
>
> Other joys are but toys
> And to be lamented
> Only this a pleasure is.

There follows a line "timber)(fishing", a line in Greek, then "Eden I.B. 1855." The letters "s" and "n" are carved in reverse.

Rosy, round faces—little more than carricatures—noted our arrival in the secluded cove. The eyes being wide open, looking straight forward, they followed a visitor's every movement.

William Mounsey, of Rockcliffe, by the sands of Solway, knew the Eden well. Apart from carving faces on the living rock of the Gorge, he once traversed the dale from Solway to the river's source at Black Fell Moss, beyond Hell Gill. He marked his achievement with an inscribed stone which, found by navvies in the Settle-Carlisle construction period, was broken up. It has recently been restored and placed on the green at Outhgill.

The builders of the Settle-Carlisle railway had some extra headaches through landslips when they sought to lay tracks beside the Eden Gorge. "Shortly after we began to tip," an engineer recalled, "a landslip took place, and the whole ground (some five acres) began to move."

Years of hard toil went by before stability was secured. The wounds have healed themselves. Even those curious round, red faces carved on rock have been softened by wind and rain. They remain as an eerie reminder of Mr. Mounsey's travels.

Corby Castle

Radiant Boy

THE SETTLE-CARLISLE approaches its termination in the grand landscape of the lower Eden Valley. At Corby Castle, opposite Wetheral, the riverside holds temples and huge carved figures, diversions on a riverside walk devised for the Howard family.

The "Radiant Boy" of Corby Castle, is a luminous apparition, which—if seen by a member of the family—ensures his or her rise to great power. There would follow a violent death.

Lord Castlereagh was unfortunate enough to see the "Radiant Boy". He committed suicide in 1822.

Above and right: Stone figures in the landscaped grounds that extend from Corby Castle to the river Eden, near Carlisle. From the mouth of the dragons pours a small stream. The huge figure of a man is from Border folklore.

Ghostly structures. *Above:* Canopy at Hellifield. *Below, left* — Aisgill box (now in Derbyshire) and *(right)* the former water tank at Blea Moor.

A BLACK 5 (44767) WREATHED IN STEAM ON THE ''CUMBRIAN MOUNTAIN EXPRESS''
IN THE EARLY 1980s.

Postscript...

THE COUNTRYSIDE of our ancestors was peopled by spirits of various kinds (some spirits being of the intoxicating variety). Ghosts and boggles, strange sights and stranger sounds, formed a supernatural world. In most cases there were rational explanations for seemingly ghostly happenings.

Fairies were reported from here and there, though they tended to haunt the verdant vale of Eden; our northern hill country weather would bedraggle a fairy's ballet frock and spatter the tinsel wrapped round the fairy's wand.

As long ago as 1857, J. Sullivan, writing about Cumberland and Westmorland, lamented the passing of the boggles. He observed: "Though it would be unsafe to declare the entire extinction of boggles, it is certain that they have sensibly declined. The boggles of the present day are scarcely more than ghosts of boggles."

The ghosts of the Settle-Carlisle are few and far between; but there have been many strange happenings to give the all-night-long vigil of railway signalmen a "haunting" quality. I was told by a retired ganger: "Quite a few of the signalmen were nervous; that is why they talked all night on the telephone. It was a weary job; you'd get the old owls squealing at night."

He smiled: "I've never believed in ghosts, though my hair rose one night when I heard a scream. It turned out to be a rabbit in a snare."

Ghosts do not exist, of course.

But — hush, W-h-a-t w-a-s t-h-a-t?